NEVER
LOSE

Heart

PETE BLACK

Never Lose Heart

1st edition

Copyright © 2021 by Pete Black & Bluewater Publications

BWPublications.com

Florence, Alabama

Library of Congress Control Number: 2021900019

ISBN - 978-1-949711-80-6 Paperback

ISBN - 978-1-949711-81-3 eBook

Published in the United States by Bluewater Publications.

This work is based from the author's personal research and interpretation.

Managing Editor — Angela Broyles

Editor — Rachel Davis

Interior Design — Rachel Davis

Cover Design — Angela Broyles

Endorsements for *Never Lose Heart*

"In this collection . . . . Black delivers a relentlessly optimistic montage of individuals who overcame hardships to achieve their goals. . . every story shares an overcoming-all-odds, underdog motif . . . ." — *Kirkus Reviews*

"I couldn't put it down. What a treasure of captivating stories that will inspire anyone not to lose heart."
> — Neal Wade, Former Director Alabama Development Office

"Pete Black is a storyteller from a part of Alabama that has known several pretty good storytellers throughout the years. Harper Lee, Truman Capote, Mark Childress and Cynthia Tucker come to mind. Pete shares his talents in a time-honored way of many of Alabama's best writers... by telling a story as though he is painting a picture with words, not oil or charcoal. If you are looking for a collection of short stories that will make you feel better about life—especially given all our country has faced during the past few years—you're going to really enjoy *Never Lose Heart*. For years, it's been said there must be something in the water of the Alabama's Literary Capital, Monroeville. Whatever it is, we can all be thankful that more good stories are being told and shared for generations to come."
> — Jo Bonner, U.S. Congressman (2003-2013)

"My long-ago schoolmate, Pete Black, quit his college baseball team and learned an important lesson from his experience: Never give up. To pass that lesson on to others, he has written a collection of columns—stories, really—that offer hope, inspiration, and unabashed sentimentality. There is no better wisdom for these challenging times."

— Cynthia Tucker, Pulitzer Prize-winning journalist

"Pete Black has compiled a remarkable collection of stories meant to inspire and intrigue us...This is a book for a time like this; a time period when there is bitter political acrimony; fear and distrust born by the threat of a terrifying disease; and racial disharmony that once again threatens to divide our nation. Pete's task is simple: show by example that great things can happen when we 'never lose heart.' I would say that the more pertinent question coming from our reading might be: 'why not us?'"

— Dr. James R. Jeffcoat, Professor of Church History at Huntingdon College

"For anyone who needs hope, read Pete Black's stories in *Never Lose Heart*. For anyone who needs to know that heart matters, read Pete Black now! You will read each tasty vignette with a laugh or a lump in your throat...but always end with a determination to never give up."

— Philip Shirley, author of *The Graceland Conspiracy*

Never Lose Heart was recognized by the Independent Press Award as a 2022 Distinguished Favorite in the Inspirational/Motivational category.

To Patsy, Jonathan, and Morgan who faithfully edited my stories, offered feedback, and made what I write better. "Thank you" seems so small and inadequate.

Jesus told the disciples a story that they might always
pray, and never lose heart.
Luke 18:1

Jesus walked the back roads and told stories that
changed lives and the axis of the cosmos. Stories can inspire people to chase their dreams, overcome seemingly
impossible obstacles, and ignite hope when things seem
hopeless. Never lose heart.

TABLE OF CONTENTS

QUITTING MY DREAM:
A FOREWORD

It's been forty years since that Friday afternoon in May of 1975. I remember the event just like it was yesterday. I guess forty years from now, should I live that long, that will still be the case? I quit the University of Alabama baseball team and walked off Sewell-Thomas Field for the last time. It was one of the defining moments in my life.

While growing up in the 1950s and 1960s in Monroeville, Alabama what I dreamed about most was being a baseball star. My parents loved sports of any kind and they fueled my dream. I spent countless hours playing ball. I quarterbacked the Monroe County High School football team and was a starting pitcher on the baseball team.

In May of 1971, my dream came true when I signed a baseball scholarship with the University of Alabama. After flirting with the starting pitching rotation as a freshman, I injured my pitching shoulder. Following extensive surgery, the surgeon's prognosis was that I would never be able to pitch again. He advised me to either try another position or give up baseball. Another position? I was a pitcher, and my dream was to pitch for Alabama.

It took a year to rehabilitate my shoulder during a redshirt season. I was stubborn, determined that I was going to make it as a pitcher. During my sophomore and junior seasons, I was relegated to pitching batting practice, never getting in a game. I got so good at throwing batting practice that I was allowed to travel to some away games just to pitch batting practice.

Discouraged but refusing to give up, I continued to work hard. By my senior season, I had learned to throw an excellent changeup. Although the injury had caused me to lose significant velocity on my fastball, I figured if I could master the changeup, the coach might let me pitch. And he did. I pitched in three games as a senior. In all three games, Alabama was either way ahead or way behind. It was embarrassing for me to pitch mop up roles.

As the season progressed, I grew increasingly frustrated with the coach for not allowing me to pitch. After a particularly disappointing loss in Tuscaloosa in early May, my frustration spilled over and I got in an argument with the coach after a game. At the end of our argument, I told him I quit the team. It was a very painful experience.

I called my daddy and told him what happened. He was shocked and no doubt disappointed. He urged me to rethink my decision and to ask the coach if I could return to the team. He told me that if I quit, I would always regret it. I promised him I would think about my decision over the weekend. And I did—all weekend long.

On Monday morning, I scheduled a meeting with the coach for that afternoon. He offered this suggestion, "Finish the season and I'll letter you. You won't have to come back your final year of eligibility." I was stubborn. I quit the team. My dad was right; I have always regretted it.

For more than twenty years after quitting the Alabama baseball team, I had a recurring nightmare. In the dream, I was always trying to make a comeback as a pitcher at Alabama. Sometimes in the dream, I would be pitching in my underwear. In other dreams, I would be in the bullpen warming up, hoping to get in the game, but never getting in. Sometimes, I would get in the game, only to have the game rained out. I always woke up feeling depressed and frustrated.

Over the years I rarely spoke about the experience; it was too painful and embarrassing. Finally, I can talk about it and write about it, but it is still not easy. I quit my dream and it was heart breaking for me. The experience made me hate quitting—in myself, and in others. It made me realize that there is great honor in not quitting. It helped make me more determined. It also caused me to be more encouraging of others to pursue their dreams, and to never give up on them.

Looking back, I can say that the experience caused me to grow and discover things about myself, which otherwise I may never have realized. It changed the course of my life and helped shape who I am. It's also one of the reasons I write these stories, hoping to encourage others not to give up on their dream.

Pete Black

THE $80 CHAMPION

*"Everyone has been made for some
particular work, and the desire for that
work has been put in every heart."*
Muhammad Rumi

February 1956 – New Holland, Pennsylvania: It was a snowy afternoon in the small town—the location of the largest horse auction east of the Mississippi every Monday for more than fifty years. Almost 400 horses were sold that afternoon. The last bidder had been the kill buyer. His horses would be ground up for dog food, and their hooves melted for glue.

Harry de Leyer arrived late to the auction because his old truck had broken down. He had driven 150 miles from his home on Long Island, New York. The instructor at The Knox School, a prestigious girls' riding school, Harry hoped to find a calm horse that he could train. Possessing a keen eye for horses, Harry knew finding a good horse at a reasonable price was possible.

When Harry arrived, only the kill truck was still there. He peered through the truck's slatted trailer at more than a dozen nervous horses. One horse stood quietly by, paying no attention to the chaos. When Harry reached out his palm, the horse stuck his nose toward him. "What about that one?" he asked the driver. "You don't want that one," the driver responded. "He has a cracked hoof, and his chest is all cut up from pulling a plow." Harry bought the broken-down, ex-plow horse for eighty dollars, all the money he had in his pocket.

Harry de Leyer and his wife immigrated to America from Holland in 1950. Having grown up with horses, Harry found a job at The Knox School. To supplement his income, he bought cheap horses, trained them, and sold them for a small profit. No one at Knox knew that had it not been for World War II this poor immigrant would have been on the Dutch National Jumping Team preparing for the 1960 Olympics.

Harry's two young children quickly fell in love with the gentle, grey gelding. They named him Snowman and rode him around the family farm. But with money tight and the horse expensive to feed, Harry sold Snowman to a doctor two miles away for twice what he paid for him.

Two days later, Snowman was back at the barn. Harry returned the horse, informing the doctor that his fence must be down. The fence was fine. Several days later, Snowman was back again. Once again, Harry returned the horse and this time, he tied a rope with a tire attached around Snowman's neck. If he were jumping the five-foot fence, he would not be able to now.

To Harry's surprise, early the next morning, Snowman was back at the barn dragging the tire. Still not convinced, Harry set up a six-foot rail, mounted Snowman, and the horse sailed over the rail like he had wings. Harry bought Snowman back from the doctor for $160.

In their first competition, the crowd laughed at Harry's horse. They couldn't believe that someone would enter an old farm horse in a jumping competition. Snowman didn't look like a thoroughbred that belonged in a show ring, he belonged in a field. Although Snowman didn't win that day, Harry realized that within this horse was a champion jumper.

The crowds did not laugh for long. Two years after having been given up for dog food, Snowman won the National Horse Show in Washington, D.C. In 1958, Harry and Snowman also won the National Horse Show Jumping Competition at Madison Square Garden in New York City. The National Horse Association voted Snowman their "Horse of the Year."

America fell in love with Snowman. Wherever they competed, large crowds turned out to watch Harry and Snowman jump. Snowman retired from competition in 1969 and lived on the de Leyer farm until he died in 1974. In 1992, the horse was inducted into the Show Horse Jumping Hall of Fame.

In 1993, Harry de Leyer represented the United States in the World Championships and a decade later, the U.S. Equestrian Foundation recognized him as one of the most successful show jumping trainers in America. Today, ninety-year-old Harry lives in a nursing home in Virginia.

REFERENCES

Craig Wilson, "Who Knew $80 Could Buy a True Champion?" *USA Today*, August 11, 2011.

Doris Degner-Foster, "Growing Up with Snowman," *Sidelines Magazine*, February 22, 2016.

Elizabeth Letts, *The Eighty-Dollar Champion: Snowman, The Horse that Inspired a Nation,* (New York: Ballantine Books, 2012).

BURT'S BEES

"Very rarely are you going to hit a homerun right out of the box. You're going go through a lot of trial and error. And the major thing is not to be discouraged because you learn so much more from your mistakes than your successes."
Roxanne Quimby

December 1969 – Cambridge, Massachusetts: Roxanne dreaded telling her father the news. After one semester at the University of Massachusetts, she was dropping out of college to follow her hippy boyfriend, George, to the San Francisco Art Institute to become an artist. Her father had expected Roxanne to get her Masters in Business Administration from the Harvard Business School, just as he had done. After all, her two older sisters had gotten MBA's.

"You will never amount to anything," her father commented then walked away. It would be more than twenty years before Roxanne saw or talked to him again. In 1976 when she married George, her father refused to come to the wedding even though it was in the family's backyard.

When Roxanne graduated from the Art Institute, she and George packed up an old Volkswagen van and moved to Guilford, in Northern Maine. They bought thirty acres of land with the $3,000 they had saved. They cleared the land with bow saws and built a two-room cabin that had no electricity, running water, or indoor plumbing. George worked as a radio disc jockey, and Roxanne worked part-time as a waitress to pay the property taxes. Roxanne was a lousy waitress. By 1983, she had been fired from the third and last restaurant in town.

In the summer of 1984, Roxanne caught a ride to Guilford with forty-nine-year-old Burt Shavitz, a local hippie and beekeeper. He had been a successful photographer in Manhattan but spurned the big city lifestyle, bought twenty acres of land and moved into a small boarded-up turkey coop to raise bees. By that time, George and Roxanne had split.

Roxanne learned bee keeping from Burt, who earned $3,000 a year selling honey. She convinced him to replace the pickle jars he used to store honey with cute teddy bear-designed containers. Roxanne figured out how to use the hive beeswax to make decorative candles. After making $200 selling honey and candles at her first craft show, her entrepreneurial fire was ignited.

In 1985, Roxanne made $20,000 selling honey and candles at craft shows in Maine and Vermont. Her candles were so popular that she hired several part-time employees to help make them. Two years later, when sales had reached $80,000 per year, a Manhattan boutique buyer discovered her teddy bear candles at a Springfield, Massachusetts craft show and began to order them by the case.

Several large chain stores followed suit. As the business grew, Roxanne experimented with other products made from beeswax. After about fifty tries, she perfected a lip balm, and later she introduced creams, balms, and lotions for women, all made from natural ingredients.

By 1993, Roxanne's products were sold in all fifty states with sales topping $3 million. Roxanne bought Burt's interest in the company and moved the business to North Carolina. Roxanne's father never called her, but in 1998 she called him. By then he had read about his daughter's business success in Forbes Magazine and the Harvard Business Review and was very proud of her. She says, "I think my ambition was a way of proving to myself and proving to him that he was wrong about me."

Roxanne named her company Burt's Bees after the name written on the side of Burt's beehives. In 2007, she sold her interest in the company to Clorox for $925 million. In 2016, she donated 87,000 acres of land in Maine valued at $75 million to the National Park Service for the creation of a new national park. Today, at age sixty-seven, Roxanne divides time between homes in Florida and Maine. Even though she paid Burt $4 million for his interest in the company, he lived in the boarded-up turkey coop until his death in 2015 at age eighty.

Pete Black

REFERENCES

Guy Raz, "Burt's Bees: Roxanne Quimby," National Public Radio, February 18, 2019.

Jennifer Wang, "Burt's Bees Co-Founder on Why She Gave Away 87,000 Acres in Maine," Forbes Magazine, Published October 24, 2017, https://www.forbes.com/sites/jenniferwang/2017/10/24/burts-bees-cofounder-on-why-she-gave-away-87000-acres-in-maine.

"Our Story," Burt's Bees, Accessed October 6, 2020, www.burtsbees.com.

Richard Feloni, "Burt's Bees cofounder Burt Shavitz died at age 80 - here's his crazy success story," Business Insider Magazine, Published July 6, 2015, https://www.businessinsider.in/Burts-Bees-cofounder-Burt-Shavitz-died-at-age-80-heres-his-crazy-success-story.

Susanna Kim, "The Unlikely Story of How Burt's Bees Founder Started a Company with a Hitchhiker," ABC News, Published July 6, 2015. https://abcnews.go.com/Business/story-burts-bees-founder-started-company-hitchhiker.

FROM SKINNY SOPHOMORE TO G.O.A.T.

*"Being defeated is often a
temporary condition. Giving up
is what makes it permanent."*
Marilyn vos Savant

November 1978 – Wilmington, North Carolina: The basketball player universally acknowledged as the greatest of all time (G.O.A.T.) almost quit the game as a skinny fifteen-year-old. He thought about it; he talked to his father about it, but he didn't. He stuck it out. He had something to prove. This is his story.

Michael came in from school, went directly to his bedroom and slammed the door. He buried his face in the pillow. He had not made the fifteen-man roster on the Laney High School varsity basketball team. And to make matters worse, his best friend, six-foot, five-inch sophomore Leroy Smith, did.

Michael decided to quit basketball and focus on baseball. He was a more accomplished baseball player and besides, it was the sport his father loved. When

James Jordan got home and heard the story, he advised his son to give the decision a few days.

Michael Jordan was born in Brooklyn, New York in 1963, but grew up in Wilmington. An excellent athlete, he played baseball, basketball, and football in high school. As a pitcher, he would later throw forty-five consecutive shutout innings for Laney High.

In the fall of 1978, Laney basketball coach Clifton Herring's varsity basketball team returned eleven seniors and three juniors, including eight guards. What he needed was height, and at five feet, ten inches, and 160 pounds, Michael Jordan wasn't what he needed. But Herring also saw potential and wanted his promising sophomore to get more seasoning on the junior varsity.

Michael followed his father's advice and didn't quit the basketball team. He starred on the junior varsity team, twice scoring more than forty points. Two years and seven inches later, the six-foot, five-inch senior averaged twenty-seven points per game, leading the Laney High Bucs varsity team to a 19-4 record and the state playoffs. Recognized as one of the best players in the country, Michael was chosen to play in the McDonald's High School All American game and led all scorers with thirty points.

College basketball scholarship letters filled the Jordan's mailbox. Michael chose the University of North Carolina which was two hours from home. As a freshman in 1982, he led the Tar Heels to the National Championship, sinking the game-winning shot at the buzzer to beat Georgetown University. Michael was an All American his sophomore and junior years, earning college basketball player of the year honors as a junior.

In 1984, the Chicago Bulls made Michael Jordan the number three overall pick in the NBA draft. During a fifteen-year career, he led the Bulls to six NBA championships—each time being selected as the most valuable player (MVP).

His career accomplishments are unmatched and legendary: Five-time NBA MVP, ten-time All-NBA first-team selection, fourteen-time NBA All Star and ten NBA season scoring titles.

Michael retired with the NBA's highest career scoring average of thirty points per game. In 2009, he was voted into the NBA Hall of Fame. ESPN named him the greatest athlete of the twentiest century. Michael Jordan has been featured on the cover of Sports Illustrated over fifty times—more than anyone in history.

"When I got cut from the varsity basketball team as a sophomore in high school, I learned something," Jordan remembered. "I knew that I never wanted to feel that bad again. I never wanted that taste in my mouth, that hole in my stomach. I didn't quit. I set a goal of becoming a starter on the varsity as a junior. I had something to prove." And prove it, he did.

REFERENCES

Bob Cook, "The Reality Behind the Myth of the Coach Who Cut Michael Jordan," Forbes Magazine, January 10, 2012.

Brian Mazique, "Michael Jordan's High School Coach Exposes Another MJ Myth," Bleacher Report, January 11, 2012, https://bleacherreport.com/articles/1020151-michael-jordans-high-school-coach-exposes-another-mj-myth.

"Michael Jordan - High School, Amateur, and Exhibition Stats," Basketball Reference, Accessed December 16, 2020, https://www.basketball-reference.com/players/j/jordami01/jordan-high-school-amateur-exhibition.

Newsweek Special Edition, "Michael Jordan Didn't Make Varsity—At First," Culture, Newsweek, October 17, 2015, https://www.newsweek.com/missing-cut-382954.

Wikipedia, "Michael Jordan," Last updated December 16, 2020, https://en.wikipedia.org/wiki/Michael_Jordan.

THE SERMON ON THE MOUND

*"Telling a man he is brave
helps him to become so."*
Thomas Carlyle

Early May 1984, Dodger Stadium – Los Angeles, California: Venerable Los Angeles Dodger manager Tommy Lasorda summoned twenty-five-year-old rookie relief pitcher Orel Hershiser to his office after the game. With his red face inches from Hershiser's face, Lasorda yelled, "Hershiser, you don't believe in your damn self! Hell, you've got big league stuff! Quit being so damn nice to hitters!"

Lasorda continued, "If I could get a heart surgeon in here, I'd have him open up my chest and give you my heart. With your pitching ability and my heart, you could be in the Hall of Fame. I want you, starting today, to believe you're the best pitcher in baseball. Take charge! Be a bulldog on the mound. That's going to be your new name… Bulldog!"

Lasorda's verbal lashing of his young pitcher was so loud that Dodger teammates later jokingly referred to the meeting as the "sermon on the mound." The skinny, struggling young pitcher left the manager's office wondering what had just happened. Lasorda thought he had big league talent. His manager thought he deserved to be in L.A., but would Lasorda send him back to the AAA Club in Albuquerque, New Mexico?

Orel Hershiser was born in 1958 in Buffalo, New York. He was an outstanding pitcher at Cherry Hills High School in New Jersey before signing a baseball scholarship with Bowling Green University. The Los Angeles Dodgers finally selected him in the 17th round of the major league baseball draft. The scouting report on Hershiser read: "Poor control, weak fastball, throws the curveball incorrectly, rattles easily, and has questionable mental toughness as a pitcher."

Two days after Lasorda's sermon, with a bullpen full of sore, tired pitching arms, the call came to the bullpen, "Can anybody down there pitch today?" Even though his arm was sore, Hershiser volunteered to pitch against the San Francisco Giants. As he walked to the mound, Lasorda hollered, "Come on Bulldog, you can do it! You're my man!" Encouraged, Hershiser gave up only one run in three innings. He became a big-league pitcher that day.

In late June, Hershiser became a starting pitcher for the Dodgers. He pitched four shutouts in July and was named National League Player of the Month. The rookie had the National League's longest scoreless streak of thirty-three innings that season and finished third in Rookie of the Year voting. He tied for the league lead in shutouts and had the league's third lowest earned run average.

In 1988, his dream season, Orel Hershiser pitched five consecutive complete game shutouts on his way to setting the all-time major league record of fifty-nine scoreless innings—a record that still stands. He finished the season with twenty-three wins, the Dodgers won the World Series, Hershiser was named World Series MVP and he also won the Cy Young Award as the best pitcher in the National League. He is the only pitcher to win both these awards in a single season.

While Hershiser didn't relish being called "Bulldog," the nickname stuck with him, and he believed what Lasorda told him that day in of May 1984. The Bulldog moniker did not reflect Hershiser's mild-mannered personality, but it aptly described his fierce, competitive spirit. Hershiser was one of the best pitchers in baseball for seventeen seasons until his retirement in 2000.

"At first I hated it, probably for a good five years," Orel Hershiser said of his nickname. "I had this young 'Opie of Mayberry' look, and now I've got the nickname Bulldog. But I owe a lot to Tommy Lasorda. He was my cheerleader, and he encouraged me to believe in myself. He made me believe I belonged in the big leagues."

REFERENCES

Chris Bodig, "The Hall of Fame Case for Orel Hershiser," Cooperstown Cred, Published November 16, 2018, https://www.cooperstowncred.com/hall-of-fame-case-orel-hershiser.

Craig Muder, "Orel Hershiser Debuts on Today's Game ERA Hall of Fame Ballot," National Baseball Hall of Fame, Accessed November 2, 2020, https://baseballhall.org/discover-more/news/hershiser-orel.

Jack Canfield and Mark Victor Hansen, *Chicken Soup for the Baseball Fan's Soul*, (Randallstown: Backlist, LLC, 2012).

Pete Donovan, "Does former Dodgers Pitching Great Orel Hershiser Belong in Cooperstown?" Desert Sun, Published November 13, 2018, https://www.desertsun.com/story/sports/baseball/pete-donovan/2018/11/13/does-former-dodgers-pitching-great-orel-hershiser-belong-cooperstown/1994910002.

THE BABY WHO WAS TRADED FOR A HORSE

"He could have added fortune to fame,
but caring for neither, he found happiness
and honor in being helpful to the world."
Dr. George Washington
Carver's Epitaph

1865 – Diamond Grove, Missouri: The slave traders from Arkansas raided Moses Carver's plantation at night. They burned the fields and the barn and they kidnapped Mary, a slave who had lived and worked on the Carver farm for a decade, and her one-week-old baby boy.

When Moses got word that Mary and the infant had been sold across the state line in Kentucky, he went to look for them. He traded a horse worth $300 for a cold, naked baby in a burlap sack. The baby's mother was never found. Carver and his wife, Susan, raised the baby whom they named George Washington. Susan taught George to read and write and to value an education.

George's job was to help Susan with the cooking and gardening. He became an excellent cook and developed a lifelong love for plants and flowers. Because George was not allowed to attend the white school in Diamond Grove, the Carvers sent him ten miles away to a small, Black academy in Neosho, Missouri, for high school.

George successfully applied by mail to Highland College in Kansas only to have his application rejected when he arrived on campus and administrators realized he was Black. Several more colleges rejected his application. Finally, in 1891, George became the first Black student to enroll at Iowa State College of Agriculture (now Iowa State University). He worked his way through college by washing and ironing clothes for his classmates.

Carver earned a bachelor of science in 1896 and his master's degree in botany two years later. His professors were so impressed with his intelligence and his passion for his work that they offered him a faculty position, making him the first Black professor at Iowa State.

In 1896, Booker T. Washington, the first president of Alabama's Tuskegee Institute, aware of Carver's success, invited him to join the faculty and start an agriculture department. Carver seized the opportunity to help poor farmers in the South.

In 1910, when the boll weevil devastated Alabama's cotton crop, Carver introduced farmers to alternative crops like peanuts, soybeans, and sweet potatoes. When imported peanuts from China undercut peanut crop prices in the South, Carver devoted his research to finding alternative uses for peanuts. In 1920, the brilliant scientist exhibited 145 different peanut products at the United Peanut Association of America conference.

During his lifetime, Carver created 285 different products from peanuts including milk, shaving cream, soap, shampoo, and housing insulation from peanut shells. Carver's research also led to 118 alternative uses for sweet potatoes including flour, molasses, vinegar, shoe polish, dyes, and rubber compounds. He made rope from okra fibers and fertilizer from swamp muck. Also a gifted artist, Carver's paintings were exhibited at several World Fairs. He made his painting canvas from peanut shells, his picture frames from cornhusks, and his paints from Alabama clays.

Carver's research received international acclaim. Three U.S. Presidents—Theodore Roosevelt, Calvin Coolidge, and Franklin D. Roosevelt—met with him. Automobile inventor Henry Ford visited Tuskegee repeatedly trying to convince Carver to go to work for the Ford Motor Company. Inventor Thomas Edison offered Carver a job in his research lab in Menlo Park, New Jersey. Carver turned them both down.

George Washington Carver remained at Tuskegee Institute for forty-seven years. He never married. His two loves were his work and helping others. Carver was often seen walking to work in old, patched clothes. It was later learned that he anonymously gave away his meager salary to help pay for the education of poor students, both Black and white.

Pete Black

The baby who was once traded for an old horse was elected to the Hall of Fame for Great Americans in 1977 and inducted into the National Inventors Hall of Fame in 1990. Carver died January 5, 1943 at age seventy-eight and is buried next to Booker T. Washington at Tuskegee University.

REFERENCES

Biography.com Editors, "George Washington Carver Biography," Published April 27, 2017, Updated January 16, 2020, https://www.biography.com/scientist/george-washington-carver.

"George Washington Carver," *Encyclopedia of World Biographies,* Accessed October 6, 2020, https://www.notablebiographies.com/Ca-Ch/Carver-George-Washington.

History.com Editors, "George Washington Carver," *History.com,* Published October 27, 2009, Updated December 13, 2019, https://www.history.com/topics/black-history/george-washington-carver.

Old Time Radio Downloads, *Destination Freedom: The Boy Who Was Traded For A Horse,* October 17, 1948.

MR. YELLOW JACKET

"Love leaves legacy. How you treat other people, not your wealth or accomplishments, is the most enduring impact you can leave on earth."
Rick Warren

August 1964 – Anderson, South Carolina: He showed up on the hill overlooking the McCants Junior High football practice field. From a safe distance, he watched the team practice each afternoon. After a week, Coach Harold Jones invited the young man to attend practice. It wasn't long before the eighteen-year-old was carrying water to players, shagging footballs, and mimicking the coach's antics.

James Robert Kennedy was born in Anderson in 1946. By age three, it was apparent that he wasn't normal. People told his mother, Janie Mae Greenlee, to put him in an institution. She ignored them. As a cook at the hospital, she didn't have money for testing and evaluation anyway. By his teenage years, James wandered the streets of Anderson with his ever-present transistor radio on his shoulder. He could not read or write and could barely speak.

Nobody was sure why the gruff football coach Harold Jones took a liking to the mentally challenged young man. Jones nicknamed him "Radio" for obvious reasons. Radio never missed a practice, and after two weeks the coach asked him to be the team manager. Each afternoon after practice, Radio hopped in Jones' pickup for a ride home.

A few years later, when Jones became the coach at nearby T.L. Hanna High School, Radio went with him. Despite the initial misgivings of the school principal and some of the teachers, Radio was the coach's shadow. He sat in on Jones' classes, helped in the lunchroom cleaning off tables, and took out the trash before heading to football practice.

Radio awoke each morning at 6 a.m. and was always the first student to the school bus stop. Over time, he was given free rein at T.L. Hanna. Everyone loved Radio. Between classes, he was the hall monitor handing out hugs and high fives. He sat in on classes and took tests with other students.

Radio's leading the T.L. Hanna Yellow Jackets onto the football field became a tradition. His halftime antics were always a crowd-pleaser. Bending over the ball like a center, Radio hiked the ball to himself and then zigged and zagged untouched to the endzone for a touchdown while the crowd roared.

Radio always refused to be in the senior player picture each year because he knew what might happen. He was a perpetual junior at the school with no plans of graduating. He proclaimed proudly, "I be in 'lebenf' grade."

Eventually, in addition to football, Radio became the team manager for basketball and track. Each year he received a varsity letter certificate in all three sports. He filed them carefully between his mattress and box springs.

Radio never met a stranger. He shared his birthday with the community. His party was always at his favorite restaurant, an Anderson Chick-fil-A. Each year, Radio needed the help of Jones and his pickup truck to carry home all his birthday and Christmas presents.

Although Coach Jones retired in 1999, his relationship with Radio continued. He took care of Radio's needs, seeing him at home and at school. Jones took Radio to the doctor each year and made sure his medical and dental bills were paid.

Radio remained a student, honorary coach, and the biggest fan at T.L. Hanna High School for more than fifty years. He died on Sunday, December 15, 2019 at the age of seventy-three, loved by generations of students. Several thousand people attended his wake at the high school on December 20, followed the next day by the funeral service at the Anderson Civic Center (the largest building in town).

T.L. Hanna has several distinguished alumni, including a writer, several NFL football players, and Boston Red Sox Hall of Famer Jim Rice. But at the entrance to the football stadium stands a bronze statue of their most famous student, James "Radio" Kennedy. In his eulogy, Harold Jones said, "Radio reminded us what was important. He taught us all how to love."

REFERENCES

Caitlin O'Kane, "James 'Radio' Kennedy, staple of South Carolina high school football team who inspired 2003 film, has died," *WSPA TV (CBS)*, December 16, 2019.

Drew Tripp, "James Kennedy, Man Who Inspired 'Radio' Movie Dies at 73," *WCIV TV*, December 15, 2019.

Gary Smith, "Someone to Lean On: How an 18-year-old with mental disabilities changed a high school football program in South Carolina," *Sports Illustrated*, December 16, 1996.

Shelia Hilton, "Listening to Radio," *T. L. Hanna High School,* Accessed November 1, 2020, https://www.anderson5.net/domain/669.

WAITING ON THURSDAY

*"Pain, tragedy, and injustice happen—
happens to us all. It's what you choose to
do after such an experience that matters
most, that truly changes your life forever."*
Ray Hinton

June 1989 – Death Row, Holman Prison – Atmore, Alabama: Thursday was execution day on death row. Ray lay awake in his five-by-seven-foot cell located thirty steps from the death chamber where the electric chair, "Yellow Mama," sat. He couldn't sleep because the prisoner two cells away sobbed all night. Tomorrow, he would make the death walk.

Anthony Ray Hinton grew up just outside of Birmingham, Alabama. His senior year in high school, he was one of the top ten baseball players in the state, but there were no scholarship offers. Ray went to work in the West Jefferson County coalmines. At age twenty-eight, he still lived with his mother and took care of her.

In August 1985, Ray was working in a Bruno's Grocery Store warehouse in Bessemer, fifteen miles outside of Birmingham, when a Quincy's Restaurant manager was robbed and shot in the head. The manager survived and identified Ray as the shooter. Ray had never been in trouble before.

The police found an old 0.38 caliber pistol at his mother's house they claimed had been used in not only this shooting, but in two earlier murders of restaurant managers. The gun had not been fired in twenty years. Poor, uneducated, and Black, Hinton was unable to hire a good lawyer. His mother scraped together money for a polygraph test, which Ray passed, but the information wasn't used in the trial. Ray was convicted, and in December 1986 was sentenced to die.

Angry and sullen, Ray Hinton did not talk to the guards or other prisoners for the first three years at Holman. He believed God had forgotten him. Eventually, under his bed, he discovered the dusty Bible his mother had given him. He read about others with trials and tribulations. He lost and found God on death row. Ray realized he had a choice to love rather than hate—to help rather than do harm.

Ray became a model prisoner. Death row became home for him, and the guards and prisoners became his family. He convinced the warden to let him start a book club. Prisoners on his cellblock read books like *To Kill a Mockingbird* and discussed them in the library.

Ray's mother visited him every Friday for years until her health became a problem. Ray's best friend from childhood, Lester Bailey, would drive her down from Birmingham. She never visited without asking, "When are you coming home baby?" Ray responded, "Soon Mama, real soon…I'm coming home mama." She died in 2003.

During Ray's first fourteen years on death row, a series of half-hearted lawyers handled his appeals. In 2000, Bryan Stevenson, founder and executive director of the Equal Justice Initiative in Montgomery, took his case. It took another sixteen years of contested appeals in the Alabama court system until finally, a unanimous vote by the U.S. Supreme Court sent the case back to the Jefferson County Courthouse for a re-trial.

While on death row, Ray had watched fifty-four men walk past his cell to the death chamber. Others lost hope and committed suicide. Thursday never came for Ray. On April 3, 2015, almost thirty years after his sentencing, prisoner #Z864 was released when the State of Alabama dropped the charges. They had made a mistake. Lester, who never missed a visit during the three decades, drove Ray to the cemetery; his first stop. He knelt at his mother's gravestone and whispered, "I'm home mama. I told you I'd come home."

Today at age sixty, Ray lives in his mother's old house. He drives to Montgomery a couple days each week to work at the Equal Justice Initiative and he travels the country with Bryan Stevenson sharing his story of love, forgiveness, and perseverance.

REFERENCES

Anthony Ray Hinton, "How I Got 30 Years on Death Row for Someone Else's Crime," The Guardian, April 27, 2018, https://www.theguardian.com/us-news/2018/apr/27/anthony-ray-hinton-death-row-a-legal-lynching-alabama-crime.

Anthony Ray Hinton and Lara Love Hardin, The Sun Does Shine: How I Found Life and Freedom on Death Row, (New York City: St. Martin's Press, 2018).

"Anthony Ray Hinton Exonerated from Alabama's Death Row," Equal Justice Initiative, April 3, 2015, https://eji.org/cases/anthony-ray-hinton.

PUTTING ON
HIS PANTS

*"Our only real handicaps are the
thoughts that blind us and the old,
tired excuses that paralyze us."*
John Foppe

1981 – Breese, Illinois: It was tough love time. Carol
Foppe called a meeting with her husband and seven of
her eight sons. Ten-year-old John wasn't invited. Carol told the boys not to help John get dressed the next
morning. It was time for her fourth grader to dress himself for school. They were not to assist John regardless of
how many tantrums he threw. Any who failed to follow
Mom's orders would be disciplined.

The next morning, as usual, John asked his younger
brother Ron Jr. to help him put on his pants. Ron Jr. refused. John screamed for his mother to come help him.
Carol came to John's bedroom, calmly told him he had
to dress himself, and then shut the door. John screamed,
"You're the meanest mother ever. You don't love me. I
can't do this. It is impossible. I just won't go to school!"

After an hour of yelling, screaming, and feeling sorry for himself, John figured out how to put his pants on. He used a technique of lying on the floor and gradually slipping the pants up his legs. It was the lowest moment of his life—and the turning point.

John Foppe was born in 1971 in Breese, Illinois, the fourth of Ron Sr. and Carol Foppe's eight sons. Carol knew there was a problem when the nurse brought a priest in when she presented the baby. She removed the blanket to discover her baby had no arms. "Well at least he has legs," she lamented to Ron Sr. "We aren't treating him any differently than the other boys. You go out and buy your cigars."

When John was three years old, Ron Sr. dubbed him left-footed because that was the foot he preferred to draw with. John learned to use his feet the way other children use their hands. He learned to write, open soft drinks, and eat with his feet. He swam and rode horses and ATV's with his brothers. At sixteen, he could drive a car with his feet.

John earned a Bachelor of Arts in Communications in 1992 from St. Louis University graduating Cum Laude. That same year, he went to work for motivational speaking legend Zig Ziglar in Dallas, Texas. At age twenty-one, John traveled the globe with Ziglar sharing his story.

In 1995, John returned to St. Louis and started his own motivational business, Visionary Velocity Worldwide. He traveled to twenty-five countries working with Fortune 500 companies such as Boeing, General Electric, and State Farm Insurance. In 2000, despite a busy speaking schedule, John earned a master's degree in social services from St. Louis University.

John met Christine Fulbright at a speech in Carlyle, Illinois, in 2002. He proposed seven weeks later. During the wedding ceremony, Christine placed a ring on the second toe of John's right foot. The couple now has a ten-year-old daughter, Faith Teresa, who enjoys cooking with John. She likes to watch John crack eggs with his toes.

John enjoys painting, especially German landscapes, and is the author of the book, *What's Your Excuse: Making the Most of What You Have.* He types with his toes, sending emails and messages on his iPhone by flipping it out of his pocket with his foot then using his nose and toes to manipulate the phone.

Today John is the Executive Director of the Society of St. Vincent de Paul of the Catholic Archdiocese of St. Louis—a charity that takes care of the poor and needy. A man with no arms has and continues to touch thousands of people. He often talks about the day he had to put his pants on for the first time. "The day my mother made me start dealing with not having any arms," John says, "was the day she gave me wings."

REFERENCES

John P. Foppe, *What's Your Excuse: Making the Most of What You Have*, (Nashville: Thomas Nelson Publishing, 2008).

Rosalind Early, "No Excuses! John Foppe Executive Director of Society of St. Vincent de Paul of St. Louis, Was Born Without Arms But Has Found Ways to Touch Thousands," *St. Louis Magazine,* July 6, 2012.

TedxTalk, "TEDxDanubia 2011 - John Foppe - Within Reach," Youtube video, 24:54, April 4, 2011, https://www.youtube.com/watch?v=FnaYjOtLzXs.

THE MIRACLE IN THE DESERT

> *"When life is heavy and hard to take,
> go off by yourself. Enter into the
> silence. Bow in prayer. Don't ask
> questions. Wait for hope to appear."*
> Lamentations 3:28-30 (Message Bible)

Sunday, February 24, 1991 – Saudi Arabia - Al Khanjar Military Base: As he did every morning, U.S. Marine General Charles Krulak knelt in the chapel to pray. He prayed for a miracle. In one of the driest deserts on earth, Krulak needed a well that would produce 100,000 gallons of water a day to support the 25,000 Marines of the 2nd Division. So far the engineers' drills had produced only dry holes. Operation Desert Storm was set to commence. Time was running out…

Charles Krulak was born in Quantico, Virginia in 1942. Like his father, General Victor Krulak a World War II hero, Charles chose a military career. After graduating from the U.S. Naval Academy in 1964, he was commissioned as a Marine Corps officer and ascended steadily through the Corps ranks while serving two tours of duty in Vietnam.

In August 1990, Iraqi dictator Saddam Hussein invaded Kuwait to take over the country's oil production. He also planned to invade Saudi Arabia, which would give him control of twenty percent of the world's oil supply. In response to these actions, President George H. Bush sent 500,000 troops to Saudi Arabia. In an offensive dubbed "Operation Desert Storm," Krulak was deployed as a General with the 2nd Marine Division.

In February 1991, two weeks before Desert Storm was to begin, General Norman Schwarzkopf, Commander of Gulf War Operations, changed his strategy. He decided to outflank the Iraqi Army. It was a daring and brilliant move, but it required General Krulak's division to move 140 kilometers to Al Khanjar near the Kuwait border where Krulak was ordered to build a temporary base in just two weeks' time.

The base at Al Khanjar covered 11,000 acres with 800 of those acres being ammunition storage housing five million gallons of fuel storage. The critical essential the base lacked was water. The drills operated day and night, but no water was found. Krulak brought in both Saudi Arabian and Kuwaiti government reps to his command post to see if they knew of water in the area. The answer was no. So, he sent word to Bedouin tribes nearby only to be told there had never been water in the area.

On that Sunday morning in late February while Krulak was in the chapel praying, a colonel interrupted him. "General, there is something I need to show you." Krulak questioned, "What is it?" The colonel replied, "Sir, you've got to see this." They drove down the base perimeter road—a road that Krulak had traveled many times. The colonel stopped the Jeep then nodded, "General, look over there." About thirty yards off the road Krulak saw a white pipe sticking up out of the sand with a cross at the top.

As Krulak walked to the base of the pipe, he discovered a large red pump driven by a diesel engine. Incredulous, Krulak pushed the start button, and water flowed from the pipe. He radioed for an engineer to come test the flow. "Sir, you're not going to believe this," the engineer smiled, "the well is putting out 100,000 gallons per day." Word spread quickly through the ranks about the general's miracle well.

Following two weeks of bombing missions, the Operation Desert Storm ground offensive began, coincidentally, just a few hours after General Krulak discovered the well. In only 100 hours, 80,000 U.S. ground forces liberated Kuwait.

Charles Krulak spent thirty-five years in the Marine Corps reaching the branch's highest rank of Commandant. In 2011, Charles Krulak became president of Birmingham-Southern College during a difficult financial period for the college. He took no salary, and he and his wife lived in the dorm with the students. Krulak's leadership turned the college around before his retirement in 2015. Today, the Krulak's live in Birmingham, Alabama, and General Krulak is often asked to tell the story of the miracle in the desert.

REFERENCES

Carey Kinsolving, "Miracle Well," Faith Profiles (blog), March 8, 2010, http://www.faithprofiles.org/faith-story/miracle-well.

Charles J. Quilter II, "U.S. Marines in the Persian Gulf, 1990-1991: With the I Marine Expeditionary Force in Desert Shield and Desert Storm," August 11, 2009, https://www.marines.mil/News/Publications/MCPEL/Electronic-Library-Display/Article/900044/us-marines-in-the-persian-gulf-1990-1991-with-the-i-marine-expeditionary-force/.

"General Charles "Chuck" C. Krulak," Awakening 2020, Accessed November 21, 2020, https://awakeninginc.org/general-charles-chuck-c-krulak.

"Gulf War Miracle," Preaching Today, Access November 21, 2020, https://www.preachingtoday.com/illustrations/2001/january/12805.

Wikipedia, "Charles C. Krulak," Last updated November 3, 2020, https://en.wikipedia.org/wiki/Charles_C._Krulak.

PHILIPPE SKY WALKER

"Would anyone but a crazed person do this? I am a prisoner of my dream."
Philippe Petit

1968 – Dentist office, Paris, France: The magazine article mesmerized eighteen-year-old Philippe. He tore the article out and stuffed it in his pocket. It was about the construction of twin towers in New York City which would be the tallest buildings in the world. At age fifteen, Philippe taught himself to walk on a wire and he vowed that day that he would stretch a cable between the towers and walk across.

Philippe Petit was born in Paris in August 1949. His father was an author and former French army officer. An unusual child, at an early age Petit climbed everything, and taught himself magic and juggling. He stretched a rope between two trees on the family estate and spent a year learning to walk on it.

In his teens, Petit was kicked out of five schools for picking his teachers' pockets and doing magic tricks. At eighteen, much to his father's chagrin, Petit moved to Paris where he worked on street corners as a mime, magician, juggler, and tightrope walker.

Construction of the north tower of the World Trade Center was completed in 1970, followed by the south tower in 1972. Petit, seized by the idea to walk between the towers, collected all the information he could find about the gigantic buildings. He traveled to Czechoslovakia to learn the rigging and securing of wire cables from Dr. Rudolph Omankowsky who trained circus high-wire performers.

When he shared his dream with the famous teacher, Omankowsky encouraged him to use a small safety wire for protection and told him, "You need to have passion and you have to work madly, to practice all day long…or you will die." Petit taught himself all the tricks you could do on a wire: front and back somersaults, riding a unicycle, riding a bicycle, and sitting in a chair.

In June 1971, Petit strung a wire 250 feet in the air and walked between the spires of the Notre Dame Cathedral in Paris. He was arrested when he came down. In 1973, he walked between the towers of the world's tallest steel arch bridge in Sydney, Australia. A year later, Petit moved with his girlfriend, Annie, to New York.

They took the subway to the World Trade Center. Looking up from the base of the tower, Petit stood in awe of the building. He told Annie, "It is impossible, impossible! My dream is dead!" Then, he and Annie snuck up to the roof and Petit whispered, "It is impossible, but I know I will do it."

Petit and his support crew made over 200 trips to the towers to plan the walk. They disguised themselves as construction workers or deliverymen. They measured the distance between the towers, observed the effects of wind speeds and determined how to safely string the wire cable between the corners of the towers. The guards ran them off on several occasions which, to the relief of his crew, forced a dejected Petit to consider alternative locations at the George Washington Bridge or Rockefeller Center for his walk. But the World Trade Center towers drew him like a magnet.

After changing the walk date eleven times due to complications, the crew snuck into the World Trade Center the night of August 6, 1974 and rigged the wire. At 6 a.m., using a twenty-five-foot long balancing pole, Petit stepped off the south tower onto a wire 110 stories, a quarter mile, above the streets. He crossed to the north tower and sat down on the corner of the building.

Dream accomplished. Then the south tower beckoned to him. In a forty-five-minute period, while traffic snarled and a huge crowd gathered below, Petit made eight crossings on the 134-foot long wire. He sat, laid down, and danced on the wire before exiting into the arms of policemen.

Today, Petit lives on a farm in upstate New York. He has made dozens of high wire walks including crossing

Niagara Falls. He has written eight books and lectures on various subjects around the world. While twelve men have walked on the moon, only one, Philippe Petit, has walked across the sky between the World Trade Center towers.

REFERENCES

Anthony Mason, "The Great Feat of Philippe Petit," CBS Evening News, February 3, 2009, https://www.cbsnews.com/news/the-great-feat-of-philippe-petit.

Calvin Tomkins, "The Man Who Walks on Air," The New Yorker, April 5, 1999, https://www.newyorker.com/magazine/1999/04/05/the-man-who-walks-on-air.

Grace Lichtenstein, "Stuntman, Eluding Guards, Walks a Tightrope Between Trade Center Towers," The New York Times, August 8, 1974, https://www.nytimes.com/1974/08/08/archives/stuntman-eluding-guards-walks-a-tightrope-between-trade-center.

Penelope Green, "A High Wire Master Touches Down," The New York Times, September 21, 2006, https://www.nytimes.com/2006/09/21/garden/21petit.

Philippe Petit, *The Walk: A True Story,* (2015: New York City, Skyhorse Publishing).

SAVING LUNA

*"Here's to the crazy ones, the misfits, the
rebels, the troublemakers, the square
pegs in round holes - the ones who see
things differently. Because the people
who are crazy enough to think they can
change the world are the ones who do."*
Steve Jobs

November 1997 – Humboldt, California: When Julia
Hill arrived at the Earth First camp, the focal point of
the protest was a 1,000-year-old redwood, which Earth
First had named "Luna." The 200-foot giant sat high on
the peak of a clear-cut hill where it was visible for miles.

Hill agreed to sit in the tree for five days. Her legs
were shaking and her heart was pounding the first time
she used a carabineer rope to climb eighteen stories to
the six-by-eight-foot platform. In December, Hill once
again sat in the tree, this time for four weeks.

In her early years, home for Julia Hill was a camping trailer as her father preached from town to town.
In 1997, she saw her first Northern California redwood
tree. Hill was so taken by the trees that she returned to

Arkansas, sold all her belongings, purchased a tent and camping gear, and moved to Humboldt.

The town was home to Humboldt University and full of environmental activists protesting the clear-cutting of the redwood forests. Hill wasn't sure what she needed to do, she just knew she wanted to help prevent the magnificent trees from being cut down.

Pacific Lumber, a family-owned business since 1885, had always followed sustainable forestry practices. However, 100 years later, the business was sold to Maxxam Lumber, who began to clear-cut the redwoods to pay down company debt. That's when the protests started.

By late December, with winter setting in and Hill in the tree for a month, Earth First leaders instructed her to come down. She refused. She had committed to saving the tree, and she planned to honor her commitment. Police gave her twenty-four hours to come down or be arrested. No luck. Loggers threatened to blow up the tree, but Hill remained on the platform.

In February, after six days of rain, sleet, and high winds, Hill was cold, hungry, exhausted, and ready to come down. Maxxam guards had created a barricade to try to prevent activists from bringing her food and supplies. They played loud music at night to make sleeping difficult. Hill journaled, "I can't go one more night with no sleep and with sleet pelting me through the cracks. I can't do it anymore." But when twenty protesters risked being arrested and stormed the barricade to bring supplies, their heroics inspired Hill to continue her sit-in.

On day seventy-one, a photographer climbed to the platform to take pictures of Hill. He challenged her to stay one hundred days and break the ninety-day record. She wasn't sure she could last another three weeks. All Hill could think about was a hot shower and a good meal. But she stayed, and at one hundred days, a local Sioux Indian tribe held a ceremony in Humboldt and honored her with a "Defender of the Forest" award.

By the sixth month point, the sit-in was world news. Hill's twenty-fourth birthday was covered by the *Los Angeles Times, Newsweek, People Magazine,* and CNN. Hill was now the spokesperson for Earth First. As her cause and popularity grew, Maxxam lost interest in trying to get her down. Still, Hill refused to come down until a settlement was reached with Maxxam Lumber to stop the clear-cutting.

On December 18, 1999, after 738 days, Julia Hill, a villain to some and a hero to millions, climbed down from Luna. She signed an agreement with Maxxam Lumber committing never to climb another tree or set foot on Maxxam property. In return, Maxxam Lumber agreed to a one-hundred-year sustainability plan. Hill's dogged persistence influenced the United States government and the state of California to appropriate $480 million to purchase and protect thousands of acres of old-growth redwood forests.

Pete Black

REFERENCES

"Julia Butterfly Hill," Accessed November 23, 2020, www.juliabutterfly.com.

Julia Hill, *Legacy of Luna: The Story of a Tree, a Woman, and the Struggle to Save the Redwoods*, (2010: San Francisco, HarperOne Publishing).

THE TENNESSEE TORNADO

*"Never underestimate the power of dreams
and the influence of the human spirit. We
are all the same in this notion. The potential
for greatness lives within each of us."*
Wilma Rudolph

June 1940 – Clarksville, Tennessee: Born prematurely, Wilma Rudolph weighed four pounds at birth. As a baby, she survived scarlet fever and double pneumonia before being diagnosed with polio at age four. The doctor told Wilma's mother, Blanche, the child would never walk again. Blanche refused to accept the diagnosis.

Finding a hospital to treat a Black child with polio was a problem. Blanche found help for her daughter fifty miles away in Nashville at Meharry Hospital, a part of the African American medical school at Fisk University. Twice a week Blanche took off from her job as a housemaid and she and Wilma rode in the back of a Greyhound bus to Nashville where Wilma received physical therapy on her legs. Wilma was fitted with a cumbersome below-the-knee brace on her left leg to help straighten her severely twisted foot.

Doctors prescribed massage therapy four times a day for Wilma to improve her mobility, so Blanche trained Wilma's brothers and sisters to do these treatments. She also recruited the siblings to make sure Wilma kept the brace on when she was outside playing. It took five years of intensive therapy before the brace was traded for high-top orthopedic shoes at age nine. Wilma wore the ugly corrective shoes for two years.

By age twelve, Wilma was the fastest kid in her neighborhood. She was a basketball standout at Burt High School in Clarksville, setting the state record with forty-nine points scored in a single game. It was on the basketball court that Ed Temple, the women's track coach at cross-town Tennessee State University, spotted her. He was so impressed with Wilma's speed that he invited the fifteen-year-old to join his Tigerbelles track team for summer workouts. He likened the style of the five-foot, eleven-inch, 120-pound runner to that of a gazelle.

With Temple's encouragement and expertise, Burt High School started a track team. In the team's first season, the tall, lanky sophomore easily won all twenty of the events she entered at distances from 50 to 200 meter.

In July 1956, Coach Temple took Wilma and several Tennessee State runners to Seattle to compete in the Olympic Trials. The sixteen-year-old running sensation qualified for the U.S. team in the 200-meter race. That December in Melbourne, Australia, although she failed to medal in the 200, Wilma ran with three Tennessee

State runners to win a bronze medal in the 400-meter relay.

On September 7, 1960, Stadio Olimpico thundered "Vilma, Vilma, Vilma!" They had just watched Wilma Rudolph run the anchor leg of the 400 meter for the American team to win her third gold medal in the summer Olympics in Rome. Three days before, she had shocked the games by setting a world record in the 100-meter competition with a time of eleven seconds to win her first gold medal. A day later she won gold in the 200-meter sprint, in a race that wasn't even close.

Wilma Rudolph became the first American woman to ever win three Olympic Gold Medals in track and field, earning her the distinction of "The Fastest Woman on Earth."

During her induction into the Track and Field Hall of Fame in New York City in 1974, Wilma Rudolph shared with those in attendance, "My doctor said I would never walk again. My mother told me I would. I believed my mother. She reminded me that triumph couldn't be had without the struggle."

REFERENCES

Biography.com Editors, "Wilma Rudolph," Biography.com, Last Updated January 14, 2020, https://www.biography.com/athlete/wilma-rudolph.

M.B. Roberts, "Rudolph ran and the world went wild," ESPN.com, Accessed November 22, 2020, https://www.espn.com/sportscentury/features/00016444.

"Remarkable Rudolph defies odds with sprint treble," Olympics.org, September 5, 1960, https://www.olympic.org/news/remarkable-rudolph-defies-odds-with-sprint-treble.

Rob Bagchi, "50 Stunning Olympic moments No35: Wilma Rudolph's triple gold in 1960," The Guardian, June 1, 2012, https://www.theguardian.com/sport/blog/2012/jun/01/50-stunning-olympic-moments-wilma-rudolph.

ALL OUR DREAMS CAN COME TRUE

"All our dreams can come true—if we have the courage to pursue them."
Walt Disney

1923 – Kansas City, Missouri: Walter applied for a job as a cartoonist at the Kansas City Star newspaper. The twenty-two-year-old was told, "We don't think that you have the raw talent to make it as a commercial artist." Broke and discouraged, Walter showed up at his older brother Roy's house in Los Angeles, California with one shirt in his suitcase and twenty dollars in his pocket.

Walt Disney grew up on a farm in Marceline, Missouri in the early 1900s. By age eight, he was selling his artwork to other children to earn spending money. His father thought his drawings were silly, but his mother thought he was Michelangelo. Walter dropped out of high school at age sixteen. Too young for the Army during World War I, he drove a Red Cross ambulance which he decorated with his cartoons.

After the war, Walter went to work for an advertising company in Kansas City. Soon bored with advertising, he quit and started his own small art company, Laugh-o-Grams, in his garage. Using borrowed equipment he created short cartoons, but the local theaters didn't buy from him. He went bankrupt.

After arriving in Los Angeles, Walter took his dream to be a commercial artist to Hollywood studios where he filled out numerous job applications, but there were no offers. Roy borrowed $500 so that Walter could set up a camera stand in their uncle's garage and on October 16, 1923 they founded the Disney Brothers Cartoon Studio.

One of Walters' first cartoon characters, Oswald the Lucky Rabbit, enjoyed initial success. However, Walter failed to copyright Oswald and lost the rights. In 1928, disappointed and desperate, he created a cartoon about a mouse that had once lived in his Kansas City garage. He named the mouse Mortimer but later, at his wife's urging, changed the name to Mickey.

Walter's first two cartoons featuring his new character failed. But on November 18, 1928, Mickey Mouse made his screen debut in New York theaters in *Steamboat Willie*, the world's first fully synchronized sound cartoon. A star was born, a company saved, and a dream revived. During the next three decades, Walt Disney Studios followed Mickey Mouse with a host of other cartoon characters including Bambi, Donald Duck, Dumbo, Goofy, and Pluto.

In the early 1940s, while visiting a cheap carnival with his two daughters, Disney got the idea for a family-friendly theme park. He took the project to investors only to be turned down. After a dozen years of trying to market his idea, Disney sold his Palm Springs house, borrowed money against his life insurance, and going against his wife's wishes, purchased 185 acres for his dream amusement park.

On July 17, 1955, Disneyland opened in Anaheim, California and became the most popular amusement park in the world with nine million visitors a year. Disneyland's success led to the purchase of 27,000 acres of swampland in central Florida. Disney died of lung cancer at age sixty-five, six years before Disney World opened in the fall of 1971. During the grand opening, the master of ceremonies commented to Mrs. Disney, "I wish Walt could have seen this." She smiled and replied, "He did."

Today, the Disney Corporation is the largest multimedia company in the world, the Disney brand is among the most recognizable in the world, and Disney theme parks have attracted over 600 million visitors. Walt Disney won forty-eight Academy Awards and seven Emmy's during his lifetime. "If you can dream it, you can do it," Disney often told his friends. "Always remember, this whole business was started by a mouse."

REFERENCES

"About Walt Disney," Disney.com, www.disney.com.

"About Walt Disney," Walt Disney Archives, Accessed November 22, 2020, https://d23.com/about-walt-disney.

Heleigh Bostwick, "Turning a Dream into a Kingdom: The Walt Disney Story," Legal Zoom, Updated June 19, 2014, https://www.legalzoom.com/articles/turning-a-dream-into-a-kingdom-the-walt-disney-story.

"Insight to a Dream: How it all began. Walt Disney's unique vision finds a home in France with Disneyland Paris," Disneyland Paris, September 10, 2015, www.news.disneylandparis.com.

"Walt Disney Biography: The Man Who Believed in Dreams," Astrum People, Accessed November 22, 2020, https://astrumpeople.com/walt-disney-biography

A POSTER CHILD FOR COURAGE

*"Keep your fears to yourself, but
share your courage with others."*
Robert Louis Stevenson

*December 12, 1969 - M.D Anderson Cancer Institute
in Houston, Texas:* Doctors amputated Freddie Steinmark's left leg at the hip. What he had hoped was a deep
thigh bruise had been diagnosed as osteogenic sarcoma,
a deadly form of bone cancer. Just six days before the
surgery, Freddie had played safety for the University of
Texas in the biggest football game of his life, and one of
the biggest games in Texas football history.

In what ABC TV called the "Game of the Century"
(in commemoration of one hundred years of college
football), number one ranked Texas had beaten number
two Arkansas 15-14 to win the National Championship.
On the Monday following the game, Freddie limped into
Texas coach Darrell Royal's office and told him, "Coach,
I'm hurt a lot worse than I have been letting on."

Freddie Joe Steinmark grew up in Denver, Colorado, in the 1950s with a football tucked under one arm and a baseball in the other hand. His father, who had been a professional baseball player, encouraged him in all sports. Freddie, who was smaller than most other players on his football teams, overcame his size by being fast and fearless.

Freddie once played in a Tiny Mite game with a broken arm, and during his junior year in high school he played three quarters of a game with a cracked fibula. Despite his size, five-feet, ten-inches, and 150 pounds, the University of Texas offered him a football scholarship because Darrell Royal liked the fight and spirit in the little safety.

In the summer of 1969, Freddie, a junior safety for the University of Texas Longhorns, began to notice a pain above his left knee. By the time Texas was 3-0 in late September, the pain was a chronic ache that kept Freddie awake at night. In early November, both his roommate and his girlfriend begged Freddie to tell Coach Royal about the severe pain in his leg, but he was determined to play in the Arkansas game.

By the Arkansas game, Freddie's limp had become evident to the coaching staff, but because he had still not complained of an injury and was playing well enough, the coaches decided to let him start against Arkansas. Freddie played for three quarters in the "Game of the Century" before the excruciating pain in his leg forced him to the sidelines. He had achieved his goal of playing in the National Championship game.

The annual Texas Football banquet was held in January, roughly a month after Freddie's amputation. When Coach Royal called Freddie's name, he surprised the audience as he walked to the podium to receive his letterman jacket by making a slow, wobbly trek across the stage on his new prosthetic leg. There wasn't a dry eye in the building as the crowd stood and for three minutes applauded the courage of the Texas safety.

On April 13, 1970, Freddie and Coach Royal met with President Nixon at the White House to mark the annual fundraising drive for the American Cancer Society. Three months later, Freddie died at the M.D. Anderson Cancer Institute. He had faced cancer with the same class, grace, and fearlessness that he played football with. His short life and courageous battle with cancer became a national symbol of courage.

At Notre Dame, football players touch the famous, "Play Like a Champion" sign as they leave the locker room headed to the stadium. At Clemson, players rub Howard's Rock as they run down the hill into the stadium. At the University of Texas, football players form the hook 'em horns sign and touch a picture of Freddie Steinmark. Almost forty years after his death, the legend of Freddie Steinmark still inspires young men to be fearless and brave.

REFERENCES

"Freddie Joe Steinmark," Accessed November 1, 2020, www.freddiejoesteinmark.com.

Jim Dent, *Courage Beyond the Game: The Freddie Steinmark Story,* (New York City: Thomas Dunne Books, 2011).

My All American, directed by Angelo Pizzo, (2015; Stockton, CA; Anthem Productions).

Wikipedia, "Freddie Joe Steinmark," Last modified June 23, 2020, https://en.wikipedia.org/wiki/Freddie_Joe_Steinmark.

THE MIRACLE AT LAKE PLACID

*"The fact of being an underdog changes
people in ways that we often fail to
appreciate. It opens doors and creates
opportunities and enlightens and
permits things that might otherwise
have seemed unthinkable."*
Malcolm Gladwell

Saturday, February 9, 1980 – Madison Square Garden, New York City: The Russian Olympic hockey team crushed the U.S. Olympic team 10-3 in the final exhibition before the Olympics. The young American squad was embarrassed. Humiliated. It was a blow out that could have been worse, but it wasn't a surprise. A week earlier, the Russian team shut out the best hockey players in North America, the U.S. National Hockey League all-star team, 6-0.

The Russians had dominated Olympic hockey for years, winning every gold medal since 1960. They had not lost an Olympic game in a dozen years and only one in two decades. They were the heavy favorites to win the gold at the Winter Olympics which would begin at Lake

Placid, New York, in four days. The U.S. team was not expected to medal.

Herb Brooks, fresh off an NCAA hockey national championship at the University of Minnesota, was picked to coach the U.S. team. He was obsessed with beating the Russians. Only avid hockey fans remembered that Brooks was the final player cut from the 1960 U.S. Olympic team—the last team to beat the Russians and win the gold medal.

On July 15, 1979, U.S. President Jimmy Carter gave his "crisis of confidence" speech. He told America it had lost its sense of greatness. Americans were disillusioned. Inflation was more than eleven percent, the Middle East oil crisis created long lines at gas pumps and Iran's Ayatollah Khomeini kept fifty Americans hostage for one hundred days. Russia had invaded Afghanistan; they were a nuclear threat and America's biggest nemesis.

Two weeks after the President's speech, almost seventy college hockey players gathered in Colorado Springs dreaming of making the U.S. team. Herb Brooks had studied European hockey tactics—a finesse game of fast skating, rather than the push, shove, and fight style in America—hoping someday to get another chance. His time had come.

A master motivator and strict disciplinarian, Brooks put the players through a brutal two week camp, which included a 300-question psychological profile; his mission: to find the best twenty players. And just as importantly, he needed to know how each player would perform under stress and pressure. After selecting his players and a month of practices, the team played a 61-game exhibition schedule leading up to the Olympics.

The U.S. team began the Olympics on February 12 with a 2-2 tie with Sweden—a huge confidence booster. Then they beat Czechoslovakia 7-3, followed by wins over Norway, Romania, and West Germany, before facing the formidable Russians.

Before the game Brooks told the team, "Gentleman, great moments are born from great opportunities. If we played them ten times, they might beat us nine times. But not tonight. This is your night. This is your time. Now go out there and take it!"

Trailing 2-1 late in the first period, the U.S. team scored a goal to tie it as the period ended. Their confidence grew. The teams swapped goals in the second period ending in a 3-3 tie. Brooks urged his team, "We just have to beat them for one period. twenty minutes. We can do that!" Forward Mike Eruzione scored the game's final goal with ten minutes left and the fuzzy-faced kids from small towns across America played like their skates were on fire.

ABC Sports Analyst Al Michaels made the call. "Eleven seconds, you've got ten seconds, five seconds left in the game. Do. You. Believe. In. Miracles." A nation needing a victory got one. WE BEAT THE RUSSIANS.

Two days later, the U.S. team beat Finland 4-2 to claim the gold.

On the U.S. gold medal Sports Illustrated said, "It may be the single most indelible moment in all of U.S. sports history." Forty years later, what happened at Lake Placid on that Friday night in February 1980 still reminds us that it's not the size of the dog in the fight that's important, but the size of the fight in the dog.

REFERENCES

A. J. Baine, "Do You Believe in Miracles," AARP Magazine, February/March 2020 issue, pp. 53-56.

E. M. Swift, "World's Top Team, the Soviets, and Ultimately Winning the Gold Medal," Sports Illustrated, December 22, 1980.

Kevin Allen, "College Kids Perform Olympic Miracle," ESPN Classic, August 11, 1997.

Wikipedia, "Miracle on Ice," Last modified October 30, 2020, https://en.wikipedia.org/wiki/Miracle_on_Ice.

BITTER OR BETTER

*"Resentment is like drinking poison and
then hoping it will kill your enemies."*
Nelson Mandela

1964 – Robben Island Prison – South Africa: It was
said to be closest thing to hell in this world. The
small three square mile island located a few miles
off the coast of Cape Town, South Africa had been a
prison for political dissidents since the seventeenth
century. The prison was cold, hostile, and notorious
for human rights abuse, especially toward Black Africans.

Prisoner 466-64 arrived to begin serving his life sentence for political treason in the winter of 1964. He was
forty-five years old. To be given a life sentence at Robben
Island was usually a death sentence. A seven-by-nine-
foot cell would be his home. There was no bed, just a mat
on the floor. There was no hot water and the toilet was a
ten-inch diameter iron bucket.

Nelson Mandela was born the son of a chief in the small South African village of Mvezo in 1918. His African name, Rolihlahla, means "troublemaker." In 1939, Mandela enrolled at the University College of Fort Hare, the only center of higher learning for Blacks in the country. Mandela became involved in student government, leading a boycott against the quality of food which resulted in a temporary suspension. He left school without receiving a degree.

In the early 1950s, Mandela joined the African National Congress, the oldest political organization in South Africa. He rose to national prominence leading protests against racial discrimination and segregation. For his actions, he was arrested in 1963 and moved to Robben Island a year later.

In prison, Mandela was awakened each morning at 5:30 a.m. by a guard ringing a bell. After washing out his sanitary pot, breakfast was served through the small window in his cell door: a small bowl of cold porridge and a bitter cup of coffee. Lunch was a bowl of corn or rice, occasionally with a vegetable like cabbage or carrots. Dinner was the same as lunch, except a five ounce piece of meat was included every other day. Breaking rocks in the lime quarry was the order of the day, every day.

At one point every Thursday during his incarceration, Mandela and several of his fellow African prisoners were taken outside and ordered to dig a six-foot deep trench. When the trench was finished, they were told to lie in the pit while the white guards urinated on them. Then they covered the pit back up before being led back to their cells in solitary confinement.

Breaking rocks did not break Mandela's spirit. His imprisonment became a time of transformation for him. Mandela's positive attitude, despite unimaginable circumstances, not only influenced prison guards and officials, but a growing number of followers across South Africa.

On February 15, 1990, after almost twenty-seven years in prison, the world watched on live television as Mandela, at age seventy-one, was finally released from prison. When he arrived in Cape Town, a crowd of 500,000 people greeted their hero. On April 27, 1994, seventy-five-year-old Nelson Mandela was elected the first Black president of South Africa, winning the country's first multiracial election with sixty-two percent of the vote.

As a gesture of peace and forgiveness, Mandela instructed his advisors to invite the Robben Island prison guards who had abused him to his presidential inauguration. When told by his advisors that he did not have to invite them, he responded, "I don't have to be president either."

Nelson Mandela's five-year term as president was one of healing race relations in South Africa and served as a shining example of the incredible strength of the human spirit to persevere in the face of unbelievable adversity. Mandela died at his home in Johannesburg in 2013 at age ninety-five and was buried in his small village.

"There were many dark moments when my faith in humanity was sorely tested," said Mandela, "but I would not, and could not give myself up to despair, that way led to defeat and death."

REFERENCES

"Biography of Nelson Mandela," Nelson Mandela Foundation, Accessed November 21, 2020, https://www.nelsonmandela.org/content/page/biography.

Biography.com Editors, "Nelson Mandela," Published April 27, 2017, Updated January 16, 2020, https://www.biography.com/political-figure/nelson-mandela.

Mike Wooldridge, "Mandela death: How he survived 27 years in prison," BBC News, December 11, 2013, https://www.bbc.com/news/world-africa-23618727.

Nelson Mandela and F. W. de Klerk, "Nelson Mandela Biographical, The Nobel Prize, Accessed November 21, 2020, https://www.nobelprize.org/prizes/peace/1993/mandela/biographical.

VISITS TO THE LOUVRE MUSEUM

*"One must from time to time attempt
things that are beyond one's capacity."*
Pierre-Auguste Renoir

1874 – Overheard in a Paris art studio: "He has no talent at all, that boy! You who are his friend, please tell him to give up painting." The comment was made by French impressionist painter Edouard Manet to fellow painter Claude Monet, speaking of thirty-three-year-old struggling artist Pierre-Auguste Renoir. Monet failed to pass along the message to his friend.

As a young man, Renoir's gift was singing. A teacher encouraged him to pursue a musical career, but he loved to paint. As a young teen, he dropped out of school to help with family expenses and took a job in a porcelain factory painting china plates and saucers. When bored with his mundane work, he strolled across town to the famous Louvre Art Museum for inspiration. In his sketches, he imitated the great works in the art galleries.

In the late 1860s the factory installed a mechanical painting process and Renoir found himself without a job, so he set up his easel on the banks of the Seine River and painted along with other artists. His work was good. His timing was not. In 1870, a two-year war with Germany resulted in an economic depression in France. Money was needed for food, not frilly paintings.

Success was long in coming for Renoir. New impressionistic art (paintings with lots of colors and outdoor scenery) was slow to capture the Paris art community. When Renoir sold a piece of art, he bought paint for another one. In 1881, after a decade of starving, Renoir's painting *Luncheon of the Boating Party* was the rave of the local newspapers. At last, he could pay his bills, no longer dependent on the generosity of friends and art patrons.

In 1891 at age fifty, when he had finally earned the recognition he so yearned for, Renoir was diagnosed with rheumatoid arthritis. As the crippling disease progressed and forced him from a cane to crutches then to a wheelchair, he painted daily at his easel. He took pain relievers sparingly, concerned that they dulled his creativity. His passion provided pain relief and a way to forget his misery.

When Renoir could no longer pick up a brush, he coached his son Coco to dab the brush in the desired color on his palette and place the brush between his gnarled fingers. His claw-like hand was delicately wrapped with cloth to prevent sores. When no longer able to walk or raise his arms, Renoir had a contraption of pulleys, poles, and chains built to bring the larger canvases to his deformed hands.

Over the final two decades of his life, Renoir's body wasted away, but his spirit grew larger. With each passing year, his paintings featured an increased usage of dazzling and spectacular colors. Nowhere in his paintings can you see his pain and suffering. He refused to transfer his misery to the canvas.

Renoir enjoyed painting his friends and they admired his eternal optimism. Once, when questioned about his good humor, Renoir responded, "There are enough unpleasant things in this world without the need to create more of them."

Renoir painted into the evening on the last day of his life, December 3, 1919. He was seventy-eight when he died, but he had lived long enough to see one of his paintings purchased by the Louvre Museum. During his 50-year career, he painted an estimated 4,000 pieces. In May 1990, one of Renoir's paintings, *Dance at Du Moulin de la Galette*, sold for $78.1 million at Sotheby's New York. Today, the apprentice who Edouard Manet suggested should give up painting is hailed as one of the great masters of the Impressionistic Era.

REFERENCES

Carol Eustice, "Despite Rheumatoid Arthritis, Artist Pierre-Auguste Renoir Persevered," Everyday Health Magazine, Last updated August 22, 2017, https://www.everydayhealth.com/rheumatoid-arthritis/symptoms/renoir-persevered-despite-rheumatoid-arthritis.

Evan Kowalski and Kevin Chung, "Impairment and disability: Renoir's adaptive coping strategies against rheumatoid arthritis," *National Library of Medicine & National Institutes of Health*, no. 7,4 (2012): 357–363, doi: 10.1007/s11552-012-9467-4.

Honor Clerk, "Renoir's exuberant canvases masked a tortured soul," The Spectator, October 7, 2017, www.spectator.co.uk.

STEALING THE GAMES

*"The battles that count aren't the ones
for gold medals. The struggles within
yourself—the invisible, inevitable battles
inside all of us—that's where it's at."*
Jesse Owens

August 1936 – Berlin, Germany: German Chancellor Adolf Hitler was excited to host the Summer Olympics. It allowed him an opportunity to showcase Nazi Germany on the world stage. He had high hopes that German athletes would dominate the games and validate his philosophy of Aryan supremacy. However, a twenty-two–year–old dark–skinned sprinter from Oakville, Alabama, would steal the Chancellor's show.

James Cleveland "J.C." Owens was born in September 1913 in Lawrence County, Alabama. His father scratched out an existence by sharecropping forty acres of land. By age eight, J.C. could pick a hundred pounds of cotton in a day. At dinner one night, J.C. announced he wanted to go to college. His father told him, "Son, get that crazy idea out of your head," but his mother smiled.

"Maybe someday J.C., if you work hard." Although sickly, frequently suffering from colds and pneumonia, J.C. was his mother's special–born son. She affectionately called him her "gift child."

In early 1923, hoping for a better life, the Owens joined other Black families and took the train north. They settled in a small apartment in Cleveland, Ohio. The children were excited to have running water and electric lights for the first time.

In the third grade, when the teacher asked the nine–year–old his name, she thought he said "Jesse" and J.C. would be Jessie Owens for the rest of his life. In junior high, the track coach sparked in J.C. an interest in running. At East Technical High School in Cleveland, Jesse tied the world record for 100 yards and set national high school records for the 100– and 200–yard dash and the long jump.

Ohio State University recruited Jesse Owens to run track not by offering him a scholarship, but by finding his father a job. It was a difficult period for Jesse. Because of his skin color, he wasn't allowed to live in student housing and had to live off-campus. When the team traveled, Jesse ate his meals on the bus or in a different restaurant. He also stayed in separate hotels than his white teammates.

Despite the hardships, Jesse excelled on the track. In May 1935, at the Big Ten track championship, the "Buckeye Bullet" set three world records. His records included a 9.4 second 100-yard dash, a 20.2 second 220-yard dash, and a 26-foot-8-inches-long jump—a mark that would stand for 25 years.

The Olympic games began on August 1, 1936. Four days later, when Jesse Owens won the 100-meter gold medal with a time of 10.3 seconds, Adolf Hitler left the stadium. The next day Jesse scratched on his first two attempts in the long jump round. Before his third try, a stunned stadium watched as Jesse's biggest foe, German long jumper Luz Long, placed his towel one foot from the takeoff mark to help Jesse know where to start his jump. Aided by this kindness, Owens jumped twenty six feet and five inches to win his second gold medal. Long was the first to congratulate him.

On August 5, Jesse won his third gold medal with a time of 20.7 seconds in the 200 meters. Then on August 9, he ran the lead leg of the men's 4 x 100-meter relay as the U.S. team captured the gold medal in 39.8 seconds—a world record that stood for 20 years.

Jesse Owens became the first American to win four Olympic gold medals in track and field. The German Chancellor refused to meet him or shake his hand on the medal stand. It did not matter. The fastest man in the world, and darling of the 1936 Olympics, had his four gold medals and the hearts of the world.

In 1996, Oakville, Alabama, dedicated the Jesse Owens Museum and Park as the Olympic Torch came through the community, sixty years after Jesse Owens stole Adolf Hitler's Olympics. Today, the dormitory in Berlin where Jesse Owens lived during the Olympics is a museum commemorating his accomplishments at the games.

REFERENCES

Biography.com Editors, "Jesse Owens Biography," Biography.com, Updated January 29, 2020, https://www.biography.com/athlete/jesse-owens.

History.com Editors, "Jesse Owens wins long jump—and respect—in Germany," History.com, Last Updated August 3, 2020, https://www.history.com/this-day-in-history/jesse-owens-wins-long-jump-and-respect-in-germany.

"Jesse Owens," About, Jesse Owens, Accessed November 5, 2020, http://www.jesseowens.com/about/.

"Jesse Owens," Athletes, Olympics, Accessed November 5, 2020, https://www.olympic.org/jesse-owens.

ROCKET BOY

---

*"How it is isn't how it has to be; it is simply
how it is right now. Your possibilities
are as limitless as your dreams."*
James Richardson

October 5, 1957 - Coalwood, West Virginia: Homer Hickam read about the Russians launching Sputnik, the first satellite into orbit, in the Bluefield, West Virginia *Daily Telegraph*. For the next several nights, the fourteen-year-old stood in the yard with his mother to watch Sputnik pass overhead. Homer's father called him an idiot. He scoffed at the idea that President Eisenhower would let a Russian satellite fly over West Virginia.

If ever a boy was destined to become a coal miner, it was Homer Hadley Hickam Jr. His father was the mining superintendent in Coalwood, West Virginia, a small town created by the Olga Mining Company. The company built the houses, the churches, the stores, and the doctor and dentist offices. Four of Homer's uncles were coal miners and his grandfather lost both legs in a mine accident. There were two career paths for the young men who grew up in Coalwood: coal mining or the military.

Homer's father idolized Homer's brother Jim, a high school football star. When Homer got cut from the football team and joined the band, his father was ashamed. He hoped Jim would get a football scholarship and he assumed Homer would be a clerk in the mine. But Homer and his mother had a secret dream that he would get away from the mine and away from Coalwood.

A month after the Sputnik launch, Homer announced at dinner that he was going to be a rocket scientist like Werner Von Braun. His father ignored him, Jim laughed, and his mother, trying to be supportive, commented, "Well, don't blow yourself up." Privately, she told Homer, "You've got to convince your daddy that you are smarter than he thinks. I believe you can build a real rocket."

Homer read everything he could find about building rockets. He recruited five of his buddies and formed the Big Creek Missile Agency (BCMA). When rocket number three flew into the side of his father's office at the mine entrance, his furious dad poured out the remainder of the rocket fuel that Homer had purchased with his paper route money. At his wife's urging, Homer's father found a mile-long barren coal flat for rocket launches. The boys named it Cape Coalwood.

Employees from the coalmine machine shop began building two and three-foot rockets for the boys out of scrap metal. Powered by a new fuel that the high school chemistry teacher bought for the project, rocket number twenty reached an altitude of 4,000 feet. On a Saturday morning, the launch of rocket number twenty-three drew 300 people and the local newspaper to watch the four-foot rocket soar to 7,000 feet in a 42-second flight. Rocket number twenty-five, propelled by another new fuel, climbed to 15,000 feet.

During Homer's senior year at Big Creek High School, his rocket project won first place at the state science fair and a gold ribbon at the national science fair. The BCMA team shot their final six rockets on the Saturday following their high school graduation. Several thousand people attended the event. Homer's father, who had never attended a launch, lit the fuse on their final rocket, a 6.5-foot long masterpiece that shook the valley as it blasted to an altitude of six miles.

In 1964, Homer earned an industrial engineering degree from Virginia Tech University and after working for the U.S. Missile Command for ten years became a NASA aerospace engineer at the Marshall Space Flight Center in Huntsville, Alabama. During an eighteen-year career with NASA, he trained astronauts for numerous space shuttle and space lab missions.

When his father died, Homer found a small box that his dad had saved. It contained Homer's science fair gold medal and a rocket nozzle. In 1997, the space shuttle Columbia launched with Homer's National Science

Fair Gold Medal on board. After all those years, the Big Creek Missile Agency had finally made it into space.

REFERENCES

"About Homer," Homer Hickman Official Website, Accessed November 23, 2020, http://homerhickam.com/about-homer.

Homer Hickam, Jr., *Rocket Boys,* (1999: Manhattan, Random House LLC).

Wikipedia, "Homer Hickman," Last updated November 22, 2020, https://en.wikipedia.org/wiki/Homer_Hickam.

THE LION RETURNS

---

*"Every great story happened when
someone decided not to give up."*
Spryte Loriano

*1986 – Burhanpur Railroad Station, Ganesh Talai,
India:* Saroo was terrified. The afternoon had begun
with excitement as the five-year-old tagged along to
the train station with his fourteen-year-old brother, Guddu, to scavenge for food and beg for money.
Guddu left Saroo on a bench and promised to be back
soon, but hours later he had not returned.

Saroo sat crying in the dark. He missed his mother,
but he had no idea how to get back to her and their tiny
one-room house miles away. Unbeknownst to Saroo,
Guddu had been hit and killed by a train.

Wandering around the station looking for Guddu, Saroo walked on to a train just as it departed the station.
Exhausted, he fell sleep on the train and when he woke the
train had stopped at the massive Howrah Railroad Station

in Calcutta. Saroo had no way of knowing he had traveled almost 1,000 miles across India. He asked strangers for help screaming "Ginestlay?" (Ganesh Talai) hoping someone would help him find his town and his mother, but the busy crowds who did not speak his language ignored him.

After several terrifying weeks on the streets of Calcutta a teenage boy took Saroo to the police station. Saroo didn't know his last name. He told the police that he lived in Ginestlay and got on a train at Burampour Station. Their search to find his town and family was short and unsuccessful, and Saroo was placed in the Nava Jeevan Orphanage.

Saroo's mother, Kamla, searched for him for months. She rode trains across India to Bombay, Calcutta, and Bhopal looking for him. Although she eventually gave up her search, she always believed that Saroo would come back one day.

On September 25, 1987, Saroo's flight from India landed in Melbourne, Australia, where he met his adoptive parents Sue and John Brierley. They flew with him to their hometown of Hobart, Australia. Saroo spoke no English and the Brierley's spoke no Hindi, but they welcomed him into their home and loved him unconditionally.

In India, Saroo's family of five had shared a 100-square-foot house and slept on the floor. In Australia, he grew up in a lifestyle he could not have imagined. He attended school and was a good student. He enjoyed soccer, ran track, and played in a rock band. After high school, he earned a degree in hotel management before going to work in his father's industrial sales company.

Saroo never lost hope of finding his birth mother, but he had no idea how to begin his search. That changed in 2007 when he discovered Google Earth, a satellite-imaging program on his computer. Finding his mother became an obsession. He worked for his father in the daytime and spent nights and weekends on his laptop looking for his mother. Using satellite pictures made eighty-five miles above India, a country of 1.3 million square miles, his needle-in-a-haystack mission was to find some landmark he remembered from when he was five.

Beginning in Calcutta, Saroo searched rail lines across India. There was no Burampour Station in "Ginestlay." He had no idea how long he had ridden the train or how far he had traveled. Month after month he searched at times giving up in frustration only to return to his laptop.

Finally, on March 31, 2012 at 1 a.m., after five years of using Google Earth, Saroo saw it—the water tower in Ganesh Talai. He realized that all those years he had been mispronouncing "Ginestlay." Then he found his house. He couldn't breathe.

On May 11, 2012, five years after starting his search and twenty-five years after getting lost, Saroo found his way back home and was reunited with his mother. No words came to her, but her tears came freely. For years she had dreamed about Saroo's return as a man.

After talking to his mother, Saroo discovered his name was actually "Sheru," Hindi for "lion." The thirty-year-old lion had come home at last. Saroo continues to live in Hobart, and twice a year he visits his birth mother. He bought her a new house around the corner from where he grew up.

REFERENCES

Greg Dunlop, "Saroo Brierley: The real-life search behind the film Lion," BBC News, January 19, 2017, https://www.bbc.com/news/world-austra-lia-38645840.

Rory Carroll, "Saroo Brierley, The Inspiration for the movie: 'My mother saw my face after 25 years," The Guardian, November 27, 2017, https://www.theguardian.com/film/2017/feb/24/saroo-brierley-lion-oscars-interview.

Saroo Brierley, *A Long Way Home*, (2014: New York City, G.P. Putnam's Son Publishing).

GRAVEYARD SHIFT AT ROBSHAM HALL

"If a man is called to be a street sweeper, he should sweep streets even as Michelangelo painted or Beethoven composed music or Shakespeare wrote poetry. He should sweep streets so well that all the hosts of heaven and earth will pause to say, 'Here lived a great street sweeper who did his job well.'"
Martin Luther King, Jr.

3 a.m., April 9, 2016 - Robsham Theater Arts Center, Boston College: The campus is quiet and deserted. Fred, the graveyard shift janitor, pushes his yellow cart carrying his mop, broom, and cleaning supplies from room to room. His job is monotonous and not real challenging, but it provides Fred with the means for a better life for his five children.

Although the job would be demeaning to many people, for the past fifteen years Fred has been happy to have steady work with good benefits. His janitor job is less physically demanding than his previous job as a cafeteria cook at Boston College (BC).

Fred Vautour was born in 1954 in Waltham, Massachusetts, about twelve miles from Boston. There was no money to send him to college and he wasn't interested in school anyway. At age fourteen, Fred started washing dishes part-time at Ritcey's Seafood Kitchen in Waltham. Two years later, he was promoted to a full-time cook position and he later became the restaurant manager. Fred stayed at the restaurant for twenty-seven years.

In 1994, Fred landed a job cooking at Corcoran Commons—a huge student cafeteria at Boston College. It was the first job he ever had that paid benefits like vacation and medical. Fred discovered a few months after beginning work that children of employees could attend the university tuition-free as long as they met the entrance qualifications. With a required minimum ACT score of 30 or a 1300 SAT score, only thirty percent of those who apply are admitted to the prestigious Jesuit Catholic Research University.

In 1998, Fred's oldest daughter Amy was accepted at BC. Fred was coaching one of his son's baseball teams when Amy arrived at the field with a bunch of maroon and gold balloons to share the happy news with her father. He proudly framed the letter and hung it on the wall at his house. With scholarship money, Amy's annual cost to attend BC was reduced from $65,000 a year to $3,000 a year. She graduated in 2002.

Cooking for 2,300 students was tough, demanding work, particularly as Fred got older. In 2001, he became the night shift janitor at the Robsham Theater

Arts Center, a complex that included a 570-seat theater, classrooms, and a dance studio. Each night, Fred meticulously cleaned the facility and encouraged his other four children to set their sights on Boston College. Fred's oldest son John was next to be accepted and graduate followed by Michael, and then Thomas.

In May 2016, Fred's youngest child, Alicia, earned her nursing degree from Boston College becoming Fred's fifth child to earn a degree there. Before Alicia was presented with her diploma, sixty-two-year-old Fred Vautour was called to the stage and given the honor of presenting Alicia with her diploma.

It was an emotional day for Fred and his wife Debra who had a child at BC for eighteen consecutive years. The Vautours created a Boston College Hall of Fame room in their house with each child's college acceptance letter and diploma proudly displayed.

All five kids lived on campus and often stopped by and visited with dad as he cleaned Robsham Hall. Michael, now a mortgage writer at Wells Fargo, remembers bringing some friends by one night to meet his dad. He told them, "Meet my dad who works graveyard shift and sacrifices so I can afford to go here." The friend was so moved that he hugged Vautour's neck.

Today, sixty-five-year-old Fred Vautour still scrubs floors, vacuums, empties trash, and polishes the mirrors at Robsham Hall. He's proud of his job and the five college degrees his graveyard shift job helped provide. "I love my job," Fred says. "Being on a college campus keeps me young."

REFERENCES

Kimberly Yam, "This Custodian's 5 Kids Attended Elite College He's Cleaned for Years," Huffington Post, June 8, 2016, https://www.huffpost.com/entry/this-custodians-5-kids-attended-elite-college-hes-cleaned-for-years_n_5756f5a5e4b0ca5c7b502a86.

Michael Levenson, "Father's labor of love puts 5 kids through Boston College," Boston Globe, April 10, 2016, https://www.bostonglobe.com/metro/2016/04/09/janitor-see-fifth-child-graduate-from-college/1XX0fLRZgXCZCgoMC2usQN/story.

Tiare Dunlap, "Devoted Dad Works Night Shift as a Janitor to put All 5 of his Kids Through College," People Magazine, April 11, 2016, https://people.com/celebrity/dad-works-night-shift-as-janitor-to-put-all-5-of-his-kids-through-college/.

AW RATS!

---

*"Never despair, but if you do,
work on in despair."*
Edmund Burke

1824 – Mill Grove, Pennsylvania: It was a catastrophe!
Returning from a trip to Philadelphia, he opened the
storage closet of his small art studio only to find that
rats had eaten their way into the boxes where he kept his
bird paintings. The rodents had shredded the paintings
to build their nests and destroyed 200 pieces of his best
work.

He was so despondent and depressed that he didn't
leave his bed for two weeks. After years of roaming
through the forests on an ambitious mission to paint all
the birds in North America, forty-year-old John James
Audubon felt his dream was dead and his life was over.

Audubon was born in Haiti in April of 1785, the son
of a former French naval officer and sugar plantation
owner who made his money in the Haitian slave trade.

Jean Audubon, a Revolutionary War naval commander, assumed his young son would follow in his footsteps; however, young Audubon suffered from seasickness and ultimately failed the naval officer certification test. It was the woods and fields he loved.

In 1803, eighteen-year-old Audubon boarded a ship and immigrated to America to a 284-acre estate his father had purchased in Mill Grove, Pennsylvania, about twenty miles from Philadelphia. On the plantation, where he lived with a caretaker, he enjoyed hunting, fishing, and developed a peculiar fascination for birds. He loved walking in the woods and making rough sketches of birds.

In 1805, Audubon married Lucy Bakewell who lived on a nearby farm. The newlyweds moved to Hendersonville, Kentucky where they opened a general store. When the store went bankrupt in 1819, the couple moved back to Pennsylvania and Audubon decided to dedicate himself to the most unusual hobby of trying to paint all the estimated 700 species of birds in North America.

For two weeks after the rats ate his dream, Audubon felt sorry for himself and whined incessantly to Lucy about quitting his ornithology project. Then undeterred, he took his gun, gamebag, portfolio, and pencils, and headed back to the forests and fields to begin again.

His method was to shoot the birds with a light shotgun load, use taxidermy techniques to mount them in natural poses, and then painstakingly paint the birds either in the field or in a small studio on his Mill Grove farm. To support himself, Audubon painted people's portraits (which he sold for five dollars each) while Lucy tutored the children of wealthy plantation families.

In his travels to scout for birds to paint, Audubon journeyed along the Ohio and Mississippi Rivers from Florida to Nova Scotia and many places in between. In 1824, he approached the Academy of Natural Sciences about funding his project. They turned him down. Two years later, he took some of his collection and sailed to England where he found a printer willing to tackle the project and by 1827, he had finally raised enough money to publish *Birds of America Volume I.*

Between 1827 and 1838, Audubon published four volumes of *Birds of America.* During this time, he also worked with leading ornithologists to write biographies of all the birds that he had painted. Almost 190 years after the publication of the collection, the 435 life-size prints of the birds of North America remains the standard by which bird artists are measured.

In 1905, in honor of Audubon, the National Audubon Society was started to protect and restore bird ecosystems. In 2010, an original *Birds of America* book, the book that almost wasn't, was auctioned at the Sotheby Auction House in London for $11.5 million—the most expensive book in history.

REFERENCES

"Audubon," Accessed November 22, 2020, www.audubon.org.

FamousPeople.com Editors, "John James Audubon Biography," TheFamousPeople.com, Accessed November 22, 2020, https://www.thefamouspeople.com/profiles/john-james-audubon-354.

"John James Audubon Biography," Encyclopedia of World Biography, Accessed November 22, 2020, https://www.notablebiographies.com/An-Ba/Audubon-John-James.

Keir B. Sterling, "Audubon, James John," Encyclopedia.com, Last updated November 11, 2020, https://www.encyclopedia.com/people/science-and-technology/zoology-biographies/john-james-audubon.

NOBODY EVER SAW A BALL PLAYER LIKE THIS ONE

"If we make the most of what we have been given, and find our own way of doing things, you wouldn't believe what can happen."
Jim Abbott

September 4, 1993 – Yankee Stadium – Bronx, New York City: He stood on the mound in the eighth inning at Yankee Stadium. For a long moment he studied the scoreboard in center field and thought back on his life. He was just six outs away from pitching a no-hitter—a dream he had imagined since childhood. He was the most improbable of boyhood heroes.

He reflected, "I am here because my dad wouldn't let me whine or quit on the playground as a kid. I am here because my Little League coach and my high school coach believed in me when there wasn't much to believe in. I am here because this thing was not going to defeat me." Jim Abbott got his no-hitter that day, beating the Cleveland Indians 4-0. It was one of the highlights of his major league career.

Mike and Kathy Abbott were shocked when, in Flint, Michigan in 1967, their baby was born without his right hand. They told young Jim that he did not have a disability, but a gift and that he was special for being born that way. Refusing to be a shield for their son, Mike put a baseball in Jim's left hand shortly after he started walking.

When Jim was eight years old, he drew a strike zone on the brick wall on the side of his house and threw a rubber-covered baseball against the house for countless hours. He imagined himself a big-league pitcher, and it was here that he mastered fielding with one hand.

When preparing to pitch, he put his glove on the end of his right forearm. After releasing the ball, he would quickly slip his left hand into his glove to field the ball bouncing off the house. Through the years, at every level of baseball, teams would try to take advantage of his disability by repeatedly bunting against him. They were never successful.

In 1989, after a stellar college baseball career as a left-handed pitcher at the University of Michigan, Abbott was drafted number eight overall in the first round of the Major League Baseball draft by the California Angels. The scouting report read: "6' 3", 180 pounds, great arm, natural cutter fastball, good athlete, good hitter, big competitor...has no right hand." Abbott went directly from the University of Michigan to the California Angels without ever playing in the minor league. He pitched for five teams in his 10-year major league career spanning from 1989 to 1999. His career record was 87 wins and 108 losses.

"I wasn't a great major league pitcher," Abbott says, "but I experienced great moments like the no-hitter with the Yankees. I made it to each level of baseball because of the people who did not give me a chance and the many more who did. Throughout my life, I wanted to be a baseball player, not a one-handed baseball player, so I had to work harder."

Disabled children came to see Jim Abbott in every major league ballpark he played in. Parents brought them—kids who were missing hands, arms, legs, or those who were blind. They brought their children hoping Jim's story would inspire them and help them understand that the spirit inside them was greater than their disability. Abbott always signed autographs until the last kid left. He answered every letter that kids sent to him stating, "I knew how far a kid could run on fifty words of assurance."

REFERENCES

Jim Abbott and Tim Brown, *Imperfect— An Improbable Life*, (New York City: Ballantine Books, 2012).

"Jim Abbott: Motivation Speaker, Professional Baseball Player," Accessed November 2, 2020, www.jimabbott.net.

"Jim Abbott," Players, *Baseball Reference*, Accessed November 2, 2020, https://www.baseball-reference.com/players/a/abbotji01.

Mike Foss, "20 Years Ago Today, a one-handed Yankee Pitched a No-Hitter," *USA Today*, Published September 4, 2013, Print.

THE RAILROAD OVER THE OCEAN

"He never knew when he was
whipped and so he never was."
Louis L'amour

January 21, 1912 – Key West, Florida: At 10:35 a.m. the train from Miami arrived at the new Key West depot. Joined by dignitaries from North and South America, eighty-two-year-old Henry Flagler, with tears in his eyes, sat on the front seat of the first passenger car. More than ten thousand people cheered the first train in history to arrive in Key West.

Newspapers referred to the 153-mile railroad extension project from Miami as "The Railroad Over the Ocean." Critics referred to the project as "Flagler's Folly." They laughed at the absurdity and cost of his project. But on this day, when at last the project was completed, civil engineers called it the Eighth Wonder of the World.

Fifty years before Flagler's Key West train ride, he met John D. Rockefeller and the two became friends and business associates. In 1867, they built their first oil refinery in Ohio and co-founded the Standard Oil Company. Over the next twenty-five years, Standard Oil became the largest company in America and the two partners were among the nation's wealthiest men.

In 1879, Flagler and his wife traveled by train to Jacksonville, Florida, the end of the rail line. They took a boat to St. Augustine and fell in love with the charm of the oldest city in the U.S. Flagler purchased several short line railroads and formed the Florida East Coast Railroad. His first project was to lay fifty miles of track to connect Jacksonville to St. Augustine.

By 1896, Flagler's railroad extended south to a small, mosquito-plagued, swamp town of 1,500 fishermen and trappers known as Miami. At the time, Key West, the southernmost community in the Florida archipelago chain, was the largest town in Florida with a population of 50,000.

In July of 1905, there was talk of a canal in Panama connecting two oceans and Flagler saw Key West as a vital port. The seventy-five-year-old chairman overrode the advice of his company's financial analysts and announced the Key West extension, a project with an estimated price tag of $27 million. No construction company wanted to tackle the thought-to-be-impossible railroad over the ocean, so Flagler did the project with his own company.

Work began at multiple locations along the chain of islands with 3,000 construction workers employed in the massive undertaking. In October of 1906, a hurricane hit Key Largo killing 125 men and destroying twenty miles of railroad. In October of 1909, a second hurricane hit the Keys with 125 mph winds, killing nineteen men and washing away forty miles of track. The following October a third hurricane washed away seventeen miles of rail.

Railroad officials urged Flagler to scrap the project before he bankrupted the company but giving up was not in his vocabulary. Flagler would finish what he started or die trying. Despite failing health, financial issues, and the death of his chief construction engineer, Flagler borrowed $10 million from J.P. Morgan to continue construction.

Galvanized by the old man's resolve, his construction team was determined to have the chief "ride his own iron" to Key West before he died. It was apparent to them the only thing keeping Flagler alive was seeing the project completed.

It took seven years, $50 million, and a trainload of persistence, but in January 1912 the Florida East Coast Railroad Key West extension was completed. The railroad line featured fifteen major bridges over the ocean, including a seven-mile bridge thirty feet above the water, which at the time was world's longest continuous bridge. Henry Flagler, who lived to see the completion of his dream, died fifteen months later in St. Augustine.

Today, U.S. Highway 1, the spectacular Overseas Highway, which stretches from Miami to Key West follows the old Flagler Railroad bed. It is a breath-taking reminder of Henry Flagler's perseverance.

REFERENCES

Editors of the Encyclopedia Britannica, "Henry M. Flagler," Britannica, Accessed November 22, 2020, https://www.britannica.com/biography/Henry-M-Flagler.

"Henry Flagler Biography," Henry Morrison Flagler Museum, Accessed November 22, 2020, https://flaglermuseum.us/history/flagler-biography.

Jerry Wilkinson, "History of the Railroad," KeysHistory.org, Accessed November 22, 2020, http://www.keyshistory.org/flagler.

Les Standiford, *The Last Train to Paradise,* (2003: New York City, Broadway Books).

THE SNOWSTORM
PREACHER

"A good character is the best tombstone. Those who loved you and were helped by you will remember you when forget-me-nots have withered. Carve your name on hearts, not on marble."
Charles Haddon Spurgeon

Sunday, January 6, 1850 – Colchester, England: It was the worst snowstorm in years. John Egglen thought about skipping church, but he put on his coat and boots and trudged six miles to the small Primitive Methodist Church on Artillery Street. He arrived at an almost empty building. Twelve faithful members had braved the blizzard but there was no preacher. He was snowed in.

Someone suggested they go home. Egglen, the only deacon there, disagreed. They had already come this far, so they would have a service. But who would preach? The deacon was chosen. Twenty-six-year-old Egglen had never preached before. Just before he began his impromptu sermon, a fifteen-year-old boy, a visitor, ducked into the church to get out of the storm. Unbeknownst to Egglen, the troubled and depressed boy was a burden on his mother's heart and the focus of her prayers.

Egglen chose Isaiah 45:22 as his text: "Look unto me, and be ye saved, all the ends of the earth; for I am God, and there is none else." He stuttered, rambled, and repeated himself for a total of ten minutes. As Egglen closed, he felt compelled to speak directly to the visitor. He turned and addressed the teen, "Young man, you look very miserable. And you will always be miserable— miserable in life and miserable in death—if you do not obey this text. But if you obey now, this moment, you will be saved."

The boy's name? Charles Haddon Spurgeon. Of that Sunday morning he would recall, "I did look, and then and there the cloud on my heart lifted, the darkness rolled away, and at that moment I saw the sun." When he returned home that day, he told his mother what happened and that he wanted to be baptized. "I prayed that you would be saved," she rejoiced, "but I didn't pray that you would become a Baptist."

A few months later, Spurgeon was baptized in the Lark River on May 3, 1850. He preached his first sermon a year later. He was a natural born preacher. In 1854, the New Park Street Chapel in London called twenty-year-old Spurgeon to be their preacher. People flocked to him preach.

In March 1861, the congregation moved to the newly constructed Metropolitan Tabernacle which was built to accommodate the huge crowds who came to hear Charles Spurgeon preach. The sanctuary, the largest in England, seated 5,000 people. Spurgeon preached twice on Sunday and multiple times during the week, always to a packed house.

During his life, Spurgeon planted more than fifty churches and was often referred to as the "Prince of Preachers." He also built two orphanages, started a pastor's college, started a free seminary to train preachers, and wrote more than 140 books and pamphlets including a seven-volume commentary on Psalms. Spurgeon preached at the Metropolitan Tabernacle for thirty-one years until his death in 1892.

Charles Spurgeon told the story of his salvation experience in January of 1850 hundreds of times. "I might have been in darkness and despair until now had it not been for a little Primitive Methodist Church and the goodness of God in sending a snowstorm one Sunday morning."

Did John Egglen know the result of his 10-minute sermon? History is silent. Most heroes are unaware when they are heroic and historic moments are rarely acknowledged when they happen. The next Mother Teresa, Albert Schweitzer, or Charles Spurgeon may be bagging our groceries or waiting our tables. A kind word of encouragement may be all that it takes to change the course of history.

REFERENCES

Bill Muehlenberg, "Notable Christians: C. H. Spurgeon," CultureWatch, December 30, 2012, https://billmuehlenberg.com/2010/12/30/notable-christians-c-h-spurgeon.

David Qaoud, "Charles Spurgeon's Conversion Story," Gospel Relevance, Accessed November 1, 2020, https://www.gospelrelevance.com/2012/01/20/charles-spurgeons-conversion-story.

Justin Taylor, "How the Snowpocalypse of 1850 Led to Spurgeon's Conversion 164 Years Ago Today," TGC, January 6, 2014, https://www.thegospelcoalition.org/blogs/justin-taylor/charles-spurgeons-conversion-in-a-primitive-methodist-chapel/.

Mary Ann Jeffreys, "Christianity Today, Spurgeon's Conversion," Christian History, Accessed November 1, 2020, https://www.christianitytoday.com/history/issues/issue-29/spurgeons-conversion.

Max Lucado, When God Whispers Your Name, (Camarillo, CA: Salem Books, 1994).

"The Spurgeon Center for Biblical Preaching at Midwestern Seminary," Accessed November 1, 2020, www.spurgeon.org.

THE LAST MAN IN THE WATER

*"What we do for ourselves dies
with us. What we do for others
remains and is immortal."*
Albert Pine

January 13, 1982 – Washington D.C.: There are not many Americans who remember the name Arland Williams, but Air Florida Flight 90 crewmember Kelly Duncan and passengers Patricia Felch, Priscilla Tirado, Joseph Stiley, and Bert Hamilton will never forget his name nor the sacrifices he made for them.

Arland Dean Williams, Jr. was born September 23, 1935 in Mattoon, Illinois. After graduating from high school in 1953, he attended the Citadel Military College in Charleston, South Carolina, one of the nation's top military institutions. Following college graduation, Williams served two years in the military before starting a banking career which led him to become a bank examiner for the Federal Reserve Bank in Atlanta.

On that particular January day in 1982, Williams, a veteran bank examiner, was in Washington for the unpleasant task of closing a key Florida bank. The weather forecast called for rain with temperatures in the low 30s; however, a low-pressure system tracked further south than predicted causing the fifth worst snowstorm in Capitol City history. With some flights already canceled, several of William's colleagues opted to spend an additional night in town, but Williams headed to the airport.

After several weather delays and additional time to de-ice the plane, Air Florida Flight 90 took off from Reagan Washington Airport in a blinding snowstorm with seventy-nine passengers and crew on board headed for Tampa. Seconds after takeoff, and less than a mile from the runway, the Boeing 737 clipped seven vehicles on the 14th Street Bridge killing four people before crashing nose first into the frozen Potomac River.

The tail-section of the plane broke off on impact and resurfaced about thirty yards from the riverbank with six passengers miraculously clinging on for survival and screaming for help. Motorists responded by trying to make ropes from jackets, clothes, and fan belts, but were unsuccessful in reaching the survivors. Several bystanders tried to swim to the wreckage, but broken ice and shockingly cold water turned them back.

Twenty minutes after the crash, as hope for a rescue faded, a U.S. Park Service helicopter arrived on the scene. Fighting the blustering winds, the chopper lowered a lifeline and flotation ring which Arland Williams grabbed and handed to one of the women. After dragging her to paramedics on shore, the chopper returned for another passenger. Again, Williams reached for the ring and passed it to a second female passenger.

The process of Williams passing the lifeline to other passengers would repeat itself five times. But when the helicopter returned for Williams, he was gone. He had slipped beneath the frigid waters.

Due to his heroics, Arland Williams' selflessness received national attention, but because of his anonymity, it took several weeks before he was officially identified. William's heroics symbolized the goodness and courage in every man. His actions not only provided a lifeline to five total strangers, but they inspired millions who would learn of the story in the news.

Williams' final actions are difficult to comprehend. It is hard to find words to describe his selfless actions in the icy waters of the Potomac River on that late Wednesday afternoon two miles from the White House. Undoubtedly, he was desperate to live just like the others. What is the difference between a hero and a coward? They both are afraid of dying. The difference is in the choices they make.

The nation's capital has many monuments to heroes—George Washington, Thomas Jefferson, Abraham Lincoln, and Martin Luther King, Jr. to name a few. On March 13, 1985, three years after Arland Williams made the ultimate sacrifice for his fellow passengers, the 14th Street Bridge was renamed the Arland D. Williams, Jr. Memorial Bridge—a Washington D.C. monument to a little-known hero.

REFERENCES

Charles Pereira, "The Hidden Cost of Heroism," *NBC News*, November 26, 2007.

Sue Ann Pressley Montes, "In a Moment of Horror, Rousing Acts of Courage," Washington Post, January 13, 2007, https://www.washingtonpost.com/archive/local/2007/01/13/in-a-moment-of-horror-rousing-acts-of-courage/7b34649e-630a-4242-a8d7-5e18a27ed6d8/.

Survivors Remember Flight 90," ABC News, August 5, 2002, https://abcnews.go.com/GMA/story?id=125881&page=1.

Wikipedia, "Arland Williams, Jr." Last updated November 3, 2020, https://en.wikipedia.org/wiki/Arland_D._Williams_Jr.

THE DREAM OF AN OLD GEEZER

*"I will persist until I succeed. Always will
I take another step. If that is of no avail,
I will take another, and yet another.
In truth, one step at a time is not too
difficult... I know that small attempts,
repeated, will complete any undertaking."*
Og Mandino

Saturday, August 20, 2016 – St. Simons Island, Georgia: One day after his ninety-third birthday, with bands playing and hundreds of people following behind him, Ernie Andrus reached the Coast Guard Station on the island and dipped his toe in the Atlantic Ocean. Two years, ten months, and 2,640 miles after he began, the old geezer completed his mission.

In 2000, Ernie Andrus' World War II Veterans group decided to tackle the restoration of a WWII LST (Landing Ship Tank) ship. For eighteen months, Andrus had served as a medic aboard such a vessel in the South Pacific. U.S. President Dwight Eisenhower credited the LST with helping win the war.

These specially designed ships could carry troops, artillery, tanks, and supplies right onto the beaches of

Europe and the South Pacific for quick strikes. The veterans group discovered that the last one of the 1,051 LST's built during the war, the LST 325, was in disrepair in Greece.

In 2000, Andrus, age seventy-seven, and twenty-eight of his sailor buddies spent six months in Greece getting the ship operational. On January 10, 2001, after forty-two days at sea, they brought the ship to Mobile, Alabama. They planned to raise $10 million to restore the vessel and return it to Normandy, France by June 6, 2014, the seventieth anniversary of D-Day.

In 2012, eighty-nine-year-old Andrus, looking for a way to raise money, discovered the oldest man to run across America was seventy-three-year-old Paul Reese in 1990. As a great fundraising idea, Andrus thought he might beat the record by twenty years. Andrus made plans to sell his house, buy a small motorhome, and begin his cross-country run. Family and friends assumed "the old geezer had dementia." He couldn't be serious.

On October 7, 2013, Ernie Andrus, age ninety, dipped his toe in the Pacific Ocean in San Diego and set out. He planned to run three days a week, a total of twelve to twenty-five miles, and reach St. Simons Island, Georgia by his ninety-third birthday. His method was to find a location to park his motor home for a few weeks, run six miles and hitchhike back to the motor home, then he would drive the Dodge Dart he towed to the next starting point and repeat the process.

Averaging eighteen miles per week, Andrus reached the Texas border late in the summer of 2014. Increased news coverage of "A modern-day Forrest Gump" brought out other runners and supporters. Some accompanied Andrus for weeks at a time—driving him out and back, providing food and encouragement.

People who heard about Andrus' run across America stood along streets to cheer when he ran by or to give him money. In Seminole, Texas, 300 children stood outside their school holding American flags and chanting "USA, USA," when he passed. On the days that he wasn't running, he spent his time responding to his 5,000 Facebook friends and answering hundreds of emails.

The crowds grew as Andrus crossed Georgia on U.S. Highway 84 in August 2016. Runners and friends he met along the way began to arrive, anticipating the conclusion of the historic run. On that Saturday morning in August 2016, Ernie Andrus became the oldest man to run across America by two decades. He received about $48,000 in direct personal donations during his run and countless other donations were made to the LST Memorial website.

Ernie Andrus enjoyed his cross-country run so much that at age ninety-five, he left St. Simon Island and headed back to San Francisco in March 2019. Restoration of the LST 325 continues.

REFERENCES

Aaron Gulley, "Grind of the Ancient Mariner," Runner's World, March 24, 2015, https://www.runnersworld.com/runners-stories/a20852698/grind-of-the-ancient-mariner.

Associated Press, "93-year-old vet completes three-year run across U.S.," The Guardian, August 20, 2016, https://www.theguardian.com/us-news/2016/aug/21/93-year-old-veteran-completes-us-cross-country-run.

Michelle Matthews, "WWII veteran Ernie Andrus turns 93, finishes coast-to-coast run on schedule," AL.com, August 20, 2016, https://www.al.com/news/mobile/2016/08/wwii_veteran_ernie_andrus_turn.

Steve Hartman, "93-year-old vet completes nearly 3-year run across America," CBS News, August 26, 2016, https://www.cbsnews.com/news/93-year-old-wwii-vet-ernie-andrus-completes-three-year-run-across-america.

SATCHEL'S DREAM

"Never let the odds keep you from pursuing what you know in your heart you were meant to do."
Satchel Paige

April 1947 – Kansas City, Missouri: The newspaper headline "Jackie Robinson Breaks Color Barrier" hurt him deeply. He had figured he would be the one. He was the pitcher who started all the talk about it being time. He was the one fans came to see in the big league ballparks during Negro League barnstorming tours. But at age twenty-eight, Robinson was in his prime and a heckuva player. They had been teammates. And at forty-one, he was too old.

Leroy Robert Paige was born in Mobile, Alabama, in 1906, the seventh of twelve children. As a kid he earned money by carrying luggage at the train station. Frustrated that he only got a nickel a bag, he rigged a pole to allow him to carry four bags at a time earning the nickname "Satchel" from his buddies. Petty theft landed him in a reform school in Mt. Meigs, Alabama, at age twelve. It was there he learned to pitch.

In 1926, with Blacks banned from playing major league baseball, Paige began his baseball career pitching for the semi-professional team, the Mobile Tigers. With a lanky six-foot, four-inch frame, and a blazing fastball that hitters described as the size of a marble, he drew the attention of the Chattanooga White Sox in the Southern Negro Minor League. They paid him $250 per month. In 1927 his contract was sold to the Birmingham Black Barons, and his salary was raised to $400 per month.

Paige played for a handful of colored teams in the 1930s and 1940s, including the Pittsburgh Colored Giants and the Kansas City Monarchs. In 1933, in perhaps his best season, he led the Monarchs to the Negro Major League Championship with a record of thirty-one wins and four losses. During one stretch, he pitched sixty-four scoreless innings and won twenty-one consecutive games.

For twenty-two years, Satchel Paige dominated the Negro major leagues, earning the reputation as the greatest pitcher in the history of the league. But Paige always had one goal, one dream: to pitch in the white major leagues. On April 15, 1947, when Jackie Robinson started at first base for the Los Angeles Dodgers, Paige was heartbroken. He figured his dream wasn't going to happen.

But on July 7, 1948, Paige's forty-second birthday, he got a call. The Cleveland Indians, in the thick of a pennant race, needed a pitcher. That afternoon he signed a contract for $4,000 for the final three months of the season. Two days later, Satchel Paige made his debut with the Indians. He was the oldest player to ever make a major league team and the first Black American to pitch in the American League.

Drawing record crowds when he pitched, Paige went 6-1 with an outstanding 2.48 earned run average in the second half of the season. He helped the Indians win not only the division pennant but the World Series.

Paige pitched two years with Cleveland before being traded to the St. Louis Browns. In 1952, he was selected to play in the All-Star Game, becoming the first Black player and the oldest player, at age forty-six, to ever play in an All-Star Game. After retiring from the major leagues in 1953, Paige continued pitching in the minor leagues into his fifties. On May 25, 1965, the Kansas Athletics signed Paige to pitch a single game. At age fifty-nine, the ageless pitcher marked the occasion by throwing three scoreless innings and allowing just one hit.

Satchel Paige's pitching career spanned five decades. In 1971, he was inducted into the MLB Hall of Fame. In 2010, based on anecdotal data, Sports Illustrated named Paige the hardest throwing pitcher in the history of baseball. Baseball Almanac selected him as number nineteen on the one hundred greatest baseball players of all-time list.

REFERENCES

Encyclopedia Britannica Editors, "Satchel Paige," Britannica, Last updated June 4, 2020, https://www.britannica.com/biography/Satchel-Paige.

"Satchel Paige," Baseball Reference, Accessed November 14, 2020, https://www.baseball-reference.com/players/p/paigesa01.

"Satchel Paige," National Baseball Hall of Fame, Accessed November 14, 2020, https://baseballhall.org/hall-of-famers/paige-satchel.

"Satchel Paige: The Official Website," Accessed November 10, 2020, www.satchelpaige.com.

"Satchel Paige," U. S. History, Accessed November 14, 2020, https://u-s-history.com/pages/h3777.

ST. JOSEPH'S STAIRCASE

*"People should always pray,
and never lose heart."*
Galilean Carpenter in Luke 18

1878 – Loretto Chapel – Sante Fe, New Mexico: The nuns stared sadly at the choir loft located twenty-two feet above the chapel floor. They were distraught. Desperate. After five long years, their chapel was complete except for one thing: There were no stairs to the loft. They had asked several carpenters to build the stairs, but none would tackle the job claiming the architect had failed to leave enough room for stairs. Having run out of options, the Holy Mother declared a novena—nine days of prayer to St. Joseph, the Patron Saint of Carpenters.

More than twenty-five years earlier, Archbishop Jean-Baptiste Lamy sent a request to Catholic teaching orders across the country inviting them to start a Catholic school for Hispanic students in Sante Fe. The Sisters of Loretto in Kentucky sent six nuns who traveled by stagecoach along the Sante Fe Trail to the church. They started a small school which eventually grew to 300 students.

Two decades after their arrival, the sisters persuaded the archbishop to allow them to build a small chapel adjacent to the adobe church and school. The nuns raised $30,000 which was pooled from local donations and mostly from their life savings. A French architect was brought in to design the chapel in the Roman gothic style like a cathedral the archbishop had once seen in Paris.

Chapel construction began in 1873 and progressed slowly. Unfortunately, four years into the project when the chapel was almost finished except for the stairs, the architect died. The sisters advertised in the local paper for carpenters to build the stairs and they had several inquiries, but no takers. There wasn't room in the small chapel for a staircase. The carpenters all suggested a simple ladder be built from the floor to the loft, but the sisters dreamed of an intricate staircase.

On the afternoon of the ninth day of the prayer vigil, a peasant appeared at the chapel. He rode a donkey, had a small chest of carpenter tools, and was looking for work. He claimed he could build the staircase. The nuns were skeptical, but having nothing to lose they gave him permission to start. The carpenter slept in the chapel and the nuns fed him. He didn't say much. He asked for no money.

It took the carpenter six months to build the stairs. When his project was complete, he disappeared before the nuns could thank or pay him for his service. They searched all over Sante Fe for the mysterious craftsman. They even put an ad in the paper trying to find out who the carpenter was, but he was never seen again.

Today, the Loretto Chapel sits at extreme west end of the old Sante Fe Trail which once stretched from Independence, Missouri, to Santa Fe. The Loretto Academy closed in 1968 and the property is now a private museum and wedding chapel visited by 250,000 people each year.

The staircase continues to amaze visitors, puzzle architects, engineers, and master craftsmen. The spiral design has thirty-three steps, features two 360-degree turns, and has no center support. The entire weight of the stairs rests on the bottom step. The intricate structure was built with simple tools: a saw, hammer, chisel, and a carpenter's square. No nails, glue, or screws were used in the construction, only square wooden pegs. Experts believe the wood in the staircase to be a type of hard fir not native to the southwestern United States.

St. Joseph's staircase, built by a supernatural stranger, stands almost 150 years later as a testimony to the fruit of fervent prayers lifted to Heaven when all other options had been exhausted.

REFERENCES

The Loretto Chapel, "Our Story," https://www.lorettochapel.com/info/our-story.

Max Lucado, *In the Eye of the Storm (The Miracle of the Carpenter Devotion),* (Nashville: Thomas Nelson Publishing, 1997).

Joe Nickell, "Helix to Heaven: The Staircase Stands But The Myth Falls," Skeptical Inquirier 22, no. 6 (1998): accessed August 4, 2020. https://skepticalinquirer.org/1998/11/helix-to-heaven-the-staircase-stands-but-the-myth-fall/.

Les Hewitt, "Legend of the Miraculous Loretto Chapel Staircase," Histories and Mysteries, January 7, 2017, https://www.historicmysteries.com/loretto-chapel-staircase/.

Wikipedia, "Loretto Chapel," Last modified June 5, 2020, https://en.wikipedia.org/wiki/Loretto_Chapel.

MINER NO. 34

*"Dear Lord, never let me be afraid
to pray for the impossible."*
Dorothy Shellenberger

2 p.m. August 5, 2010 – Copiapo, Chile: The 120-year-old San Jose gold and copper mine twenty-eight miles north of Copiapo, Chile, had been groaning for several months. Management reassured miners that everything was safe, but at 2 p.m. on that Thursday afternoon, hundreds of tons of rock collapsed, effectively sealing the mineshaft and trapping thirty-three men a half-mile beneath the earth's surface.

A few hours after the dust settled, all the trapped miners made it to a sixteen-by-fourteen-foot safe zone at the 2,300-foot level. Amazingly none were injured. The mine collapse destroyed the electrical, ventilation, water, and communication systems, leaving the miners with only a small amount of food and water, a rudimentary lighting arrangement, and no communication with the outside world. As they assessed the situation, one miner voiced what everyone was secretly thinking, "We're screwed."

The one exception was Jose Henriquez, a veteran miner with more than thirty years of experience. He was the shift's equipment operator and labor supervisor. Despite having only been at the mine for seven months, Henriquez's knowledge of mining, his strong Christian faith, and his positive attitude had gained him the respect of his coworkers.

Several days before the disaster, Henriquez's grandmother had shared a premonition that something bad was about to happen, but that everything would be ok. Late in the afternoon of August 5, as fear was settling in, the miners chose Henriquez to be their spiritual leader and asked him to pray. God was their only hope.

Henriquez led daily prayer meetings at noon and 6 p.m. He prayed for unity among the miners and for God's will to be done. With a faith strengthened by his grandmother's words, he prayed for the impossible. Confidence grew that they would be rescued. God's presence was so apparent that the miners began to refer to Him as Miner No. 34.

With communication lines down, the miners had no idea how hopeless their situation appeared from the surface. Mine officials knew the odds were slim that any miners had survived. It was determined a single block of rock, estimated to weigh 800,000 tons, had broken off and fallen through the layers of the mine causing a chain reaction.

Knowing that any survivors would be at the 2,300-foot level safe zone, rescuers attempted to drill a small hole to the chamber. Hitting a classroom-size cavity from a half-mile away proved to be no easy task. It took eight tries, but on day seventeen the drill bit broke through the chamber roof.

When a note with the message, "We are well in the refuge, the 33," was found attached to the drill bit, shouts of jubilation erupted from 2,000 friends and family members. They had prayed and waited for two and a half weeks under the tent at the makeshift Camp Hope located near the mine's entrance.

A larger hole was drilled to provide food, water, and medical supplies to the trapped miners. When officials brought in a psychologist to provide counseling via phone, they were informed counseling wasn't necessary—Miner No. 34 was on the job. The next challenge was to drill a 28-inch diameter hole large enough to pass a capsule through to extract the miners without creating further instability in the fragile rock column. The world watched and waited as a NASA team designed and built the rescue capsule and mine rescue teams around the world joined in the effort.

On October 13, 2005, seven weeks after the miners were discovered alive and sixty-nine days after the collapse, thirty-three miners were brought to the surface one-at-a-time. As they emerged from the hole, all were wearing "Thank you, Lord" t-shirts which had been supplied by a church. A mine tragedy that buried thirty-three men a half-mile underground for more than two months became a global story of faith, courage, teamwork, and perseverance against overwhelming odds.

REFERENCES

Adam Bledford, Patrick Johnson and Anna Jones, "As It Happened: Chile Mine Disaster—Minute by Minute Coverage," BBC News, August, September, October 2010.

Amy Edmondson, "How 'Teaming' Saved 33 Lives in the Chilean Mining Disaster," Harvard Business School, January 29, 2018, https://hbswk.hbs.edu/item/how-teaming-saved-33-lives-in-the-chilean-mining-disaster.

Kyle Idleman, "Four Degrees of Desperation," Sermon at Southeast Christian Church, Louisville, May 15, 2015.

Trisha Thadani, "Relive the moments: 33 Chilean miners rescued alive 5 years ago," USA Today, October 13, 2015, https://www.usatoday.com/story/news/2015/10/13/chilean-miners-resuce/73838496/.

THE WINNER WITHIN

"The task of leadership is not to put greatness into people, but to elicit it. The greatness is already there."
John Buchan

July 1959 – Green Bay Packer Football Camp, Green Bay, Wisconsin: On a hot afternoon during the first week of the grueling two-a-day practices, fiery new head coach Vince Lombardi stopped practice and walked over to second-year guard Jerry Kramer who had once again jumped off sides.

With his face six inches from Kramer's nose, Lombardi screamed, "The concentration period for a college student is five minutes, in high school it's three minutes, in kindergarten it's thirty seconds. And you...*bleep* you don't even have that! So where the *bleep* does that *bleeping* put you mister? Get your *bleeping bleep* off this field!"

Kramer wiped Lombardi's spray from his face and began the long walk to the locker room wondering if he still had a place on the team. After practice, Lombardi wandered through the locker room to find Kramer still in his uniform sitting at his locker with his head down, eyes all liquid.

Lombardi sat down beside the young guard, put his hand on his shoulder, and told Kramer, "This afternoon you were a lousy football player, but you can become one of the best guards in the National Football League."

Coach Lombardi had inherited a laughing-stock football franchise. Prior to his arrival, the Packers had nine straight losing seasons and the year before he arrived, they won only one game. But over the next decade under Lombardi, the Packers won five NFL Championships including an unprecedented three-in-a-row from 1965 to 1967. Jerry Kramer was at right guard for all of them. He was selected to the NFL All Pro Team six times. In 1969, he was honored as the Best Guard in the First 50 Years of the NFL.

Following his retirement in 1968, Kramer was asked about his career and Vince Lombardi. He responded, "The turning point was that hot afternoon in 1959 when Lombardi put his arm around me after a very difficult practice and told me that I could become one of the best guards in football. That statement gave me a new feeling about myself. The positive reinforcement by him at that moment changed my whole career."

On Saturday, February 3, 2018, Jerry Kramer, his wife, two children, and a grandchild were in Minneapolis, Minnesota, to attend the Super Bowl LII; but more importantly Kramer's name was on the NFL Hall of Fame ballot. It was his eleventh time on the ballot and the annual trip had become painful. He told everyone making the Hall of Fame was no big deal, but he was fooling no one.

Kramer knew the drill. He was to remain in his hotel room where he would be notified of the outcome between 3 and 4 p.m. His family waited anxiously in the room with him. At 3:30, there was a knock at the door. Kramer answered the door to find a wide-eyed maid. His hopes sunk with each passing minute. By 3:40, he had resigned himself for the usual outcome.

Five more minutes passed when suddenly there was a loud pounding on the door. The entire family stood and a breathless Kramer opened the door. David Baker, President of the Pro Football Hall of Fame, surrounded by six reporters taking pictures, gave him thumbs up. Kramer, eyes teary and voice quivering, told six-foot, nine-inch, 400-pound Baker, "You're the most beautiful man I have ever seen."

Forty-five years after becoming eligible, on August 5, 2018, eighty-two-year-old Jerry Kramer was enshrined in the Pro Football Hall of Fame in Canton, Ohio. He will be the final member of the NFL fiftieth anniversary team to be inducted.

REFERENCES

Andy Benoit, "Anxious Waiting, and then Finally, a Knock at the Door: With Jerry Kramer with His Call to the Hall," *Sports Illustrated*, February 4, 2018.

Bob Fox, "Jerry Kramer Reflects on his Induction into the Pro Football Hall of Fame," Bob Fox (blog), February 8, 2018, https://greenbaybobfox.wordpress.com/2018/02/08/jerry-kramer-reflects-on-his-induction-into-the-pro-football-hall-of-fame.

Jerry Kramer, Accessed November 22, 2020, www.jerrykramer.com.

Jerry Kramer, *Instant Replay: The Green Bay Diary of Jerry Kramer*, (2008: New York City, Vintage Books).

TINKERBELLE

"There is a time when one must decide either to risk everything to fulfill one's dreams or sit for the rest of one's life in the backyard."
Robert Manry

June 1, 1965 – Falmouth, Massachusetts: The thirteen-foot sailboat *Tinkerbelle* quietly set sail for its destination 3,200 miles away in Falmouth, England. If successful, it would be the smallest sailboat to cross the Atlantic Ocean. At the helm was Robert Manry, a copy editor who was bored with his job at the Cleveland, Ohio *Plain Dealer* newspaper.

Manry learned to sail as a boy while growing up in India. After reading Josh Slocumb's book *Sailing Alone Around the World*, he became fascinated with the idea of sailing around the world. In 1959, Manry saw an ad for a thirty-year-old, thirteen-foot whitecap class sailboat and he bought it for $160.

He rebuilt the boat and pulled it behind the family station wagon to lakes in Ohio and Pennsylvania on summer vacations. For three decades, Manry quietly dreamed of sailing across the Atlantic. On his forty-seventh birthday, he took a three-month sabbatical from his job and decided to give it a try.

Manry was afraid, not of the ocean, but that people would try to talk him out of his crazy idea. He only told his wife, Virginia, and a few close relatives about the trip. As he shoved off from the Falmouth marina, Manry handed the harbormaster a letter addressed to his newspaper employees informing them that he was sailing to England. The stories began appearing in the *Plain Dealer* paper just a couple of days after his departure. They were a hit with readers and soon other newspapers around the country took a keen interest in Manry's trip.

By the third night, panic had replaced boredom as Manry maneuvered his little boat across busy shipping lanes trying not to capsize. He tried to sleep in the daytime and sail at night when ships might not see his tiny sailboat. On six occasions storms swept him overboard and a rope tied around his waist was the only thing that saved him. Another storm knocked out the radar. Three times Manry repaired a broken rudder. On his best day, he sailed eighty-seven miles. On other days, *Tinkerbelle* sat still on a windless ocean.

During the last leg of the journey, *Tinkerbelle* was reported lost. Royal Air Force planes were dispatched to search for Manry but after twenty-four hours there was still no word on Manry's location. Family and friends in

New England feared the worst, but on the second day a search plane spotted the little sailboat.

Robert Manry had no idea that his adventure had become a major story on both sides of the Atlantic. He had left Massachusetts with no fanfare and expected nothing more when he arrived. Tired, cold, forty pounds lighter, and sleep deprived, Manry simply planned to get a hotel room, a hot shower, and a good meal. The next day he would contact the Associated Press to see if there was interest in his story.

On Tuesday, August 17 in the late afternoon, seventy-eight days after setting sail, *Tinkerbelle* finally began the approach into Falmouth Harbor. To Manry's amazement, pandemonium greeted his arrival. He agreed to be towed to port due to the congestion created by more than 300 vessels, most with horns blasting that had jammed the harbor anticipating his arrival. An estimated 50,000 people waited at the docks to celebrate the modern-day Charles Lindberg. Manry's newspaper had flown his wife and their two children over for the event. Every major paper on both sides of the Atlantic was there to cover the story.

Robert Manry never returned to his job at the newspaper. Instead, he captured his adventure in a successful book, wrote for magazines, and gave lectures around the country. He died five years later at age fifty-two of a heart attack.

REFERENCES

Cecelia Hartman, "Epilogue," ClevelandMemory.org, Accessed November 22, 2020, http://www.clevelandmemory.org/ebooks/tinkerbelle/tinkepilogue.

Robert Manry, *Tinkerbelle: The Story of the Smallest Boat Ever to Cross the Atlantic Nonstop*, (1966: New York City, Harper & Row Publishing).

The Robert Manry Project, Accessed November 22, 2020, www.robertmanryproject.com.

DON'T LET THEM BREAK THROUGH

"Never, never, never, never, in nothing great or small, large or petty, never give in, except to convictions of honor or good sense. Never yield to force. Never yield to the apparently overwhelming might of the enemy."
Winston Churchill

Friday, July 3, 1863 – Gettysburg, Pennsylvania: It was a hot, sultry afternoon. Joshua Chamberlain and the 20th Maine Regiment were positioned on Little Round Top, a hill at the extreme left end of a line of 80,000 Union soldiers that stretched out three miles to Gettysburg. A year earlier, Chamberlain, at thirty-four years old, had been a professor at Bowdoin College in Maine. On this afternoon, he was the colonel in charge of the 20th Maine.

Chamberlain's unit had formed in the summer of 1862 with almost 1,000 volunteers. A year later they joined General Meade in southern Pennsylvania. After marching one hundred miles in five days in the hottest weather any of them had ever seen, the 20th Maine reached their position at Little Round Top at midnight two days before.

Chamberlain's orders were to defend the position, the highest point on the battlefield, at all costs. "You cannot withdraw under any conditions," he had been commanded. Chamberlain understood that if he let the Rebels break through the battle might be lost. He could not retreat, and he knew it.

All day Thursday the fighting was fierce. Casualties were high and Chamberlain was concerned that another day like that would decimate his remaining 300 men. They awoke Friday morning exhausted and hungry, their meager food rations gone.

At 3 p.m. on Friday afternoon the Alabama 15th and 47th Regiments made a charge up Little Round Top. Chamberlain's men were positioned behind a 100-yard-long low rock wall they had built. The 20th Maine stopped the Rebel charge only to face a second charge, a third, and then a fourth charge. As the sun set, the Rebels were regrouping at the bottom of the hill.

The 20th Maine was down to roughly 200 soldiers and they were low on ammunition. First Sergeant Ellis Spear approached Chamberlain and reported, "Colonel, they are forming again, we've lost almost a third of the men, we're almost out of ammo." Spear suggested they consider pulling out. Chamberlain replied, "Take ammunition from the wounded. Not pulling out, carry out the order!" Spear shouted, "If they come again, you know we won't hold 'em."

Chamberlain paused while Spear and several officers awaited his decision. Chamberlain looked from face to face. If he retreated the hill was gone. After a long moment, Chamberlain shouted, "Fix bayonets...Charge!" At first, the men stared at him in disbelief. But then they began jumping the wall, stepping over the bodies of the dead, and screaming like wild animals as they charged down the hill.

Chamberlain watched as the Rebels turned and ran back down the hill. They were surprised and uncertain about what was happening. Assuming Union reinforcements had arrived, the Rebel soldiers surrendered. As night fell, the 20th Maine, with help from the 83rd Pennsylvania regiment, captured about 400 confederate soldiers.

For 150 years, historians have debated the importance of Little Round Top to the Union victory at Gettysburg. Some believe that the Pennsylvania battlefield was the turning point in the Civil War. They believe that if the Rebels had broken through the Confederate Army would have won at battle. And with that victory, historians believe the South might have won the Civil War.

Colonel Joshua Chamberlain knew his position at Little Round Top was a critical one, but he could not have imagined the potential implications of carrying out his orders and not giving up on that July afternoon. Like Chamberlain, we may never know the consequences of our decisions when we choose not to give up, when we choose to persevere even when the odds seem overwhelming!

REFERENCES

Andy Andrews, *The Butterfly Effect – How Your Life Matters*, (Scotland: Thomas Nelson Publishing, 2010).

Michael Shaara, *The Killer Angels – The Classic Novel of the Civil War (The Civil War 1861-1865 Book 2)*, (New York City: Ballantine Books, 1987).

ENCOURAGEMENT

"The power of words is immense. A well-chosen word has often sufficed to stop a flying army, to change defeat into victory, and to save an empire."
Emile De Girardin

February 26, 1791 – London, England: Methodist theologian John Wesley penned a letter to his good friend William Wilberforce in the faith. In failing health at age eighty-eight, it was the last letter Wesley ever wrote. As a longtime outspoken opponent of the British Slave Trade, he wrote to encourage Wilberforce to continue his valiant fight in the English Parliament against slavery. Four days after writing the letter, Wesley died. The message read:

> *Dear Sir:*
> *Unless the divine power has raised you up, I see not how you can go through your glorious enterprise, in opposing that execrable villainy, which is the scandal of religion, of England, and of human nature. Oh, be not weary in well doing! Go*

on, in the name of God and in the power of His might, till even American slavery (the vilest that ever saw the sun) shall vanish away before it. That He who has guided you from your youth, may continue to strengthen you in this and all things, is the prayer of,
Your affectionate servant,
J. Wesley

William Wilberforce was born in Hull, England, in 1759, and at age seventeen entered Cambridge University. In 1780, while still a student at Cambridge, he was elected a member of the House of Commons representing Hull. Although slavery had been legal in the British Isles for more than a hundred years, Wilberforce became more attuned to the appalling practices of African slavery following his conversion to Christianity in 1785.

When Wilberforce received Wesley's letter, he was once again facing a discouraging defeat in his attempt to abolish Britain's slave trade. Wilberforce had delivered an impassioned four hour speech against slavery to the House of Commons in Parliament only to have his bill soundly defeated 163 to 88. Wesley's letter not only encouraged him to continue the fight that spring of 1791, but it was an inspiration to him for the remainder of his life.

In May 1789, Wilberforce introduced twelve resolutions to Parliament condemning the "morally reprehensible" treatment of Africans, particularly on slave ships. British cargo ships carried goods from England to Africa and transported slaves, who were chained and often stacked like logs for shipping purposes, to the West Indies. Then the ships sailed to England with slave-grown products like sugar, tobacco, and cotton.

With eighty percent of England's foreign income based on the slave trade, Wilberforce frequently encountered violent opposition to his resolutions. Although vilified by his colleagues, Wilberforce introduced anti-slavery bills every year from 1792 until the end of the decade. In 1804, Wilberforce successfully had a law passed in the House of Commons only to see it defeated in the House of Lords. Finally, on March 25, 1806, after eighteen years of speeches and legislation on the part of William Wilberforce, Parliament passed the Slave Trade Act.

Although the Slave Trade Act was passed, slavery did not go away. The law was not strictly enforced and many slave traders ignored it completely. Wilberforce still continued his campaign, giving his final anti-slavery speech in April 1833 three months before his death on July 29, 1833. Two days after his death, and forty-four years after he had given his first anti-slavery speech, Parliament, in a salute to William Wilberforce, passed a law abolishing slavery forever in England and freeing 800,000 slaves.

Although he did not live to see the realization of his dream, no one was more responsible for the abolition of slavery in the British Empire than William Wilberforce.

On numerous occasions, Wilberforce almost gave up the fight. But every time he became discouraged, he read Wesley's letter and Wesley's words never failed to encourage and strengthen him to continue the fight.

REFERENCES

Encyclopedia Britannica's Editors, "John Wesley: English clergyman," *Britannica*, Published July 20, 1998, Updated July 13, 2020, https://www.britannica.com/biography/John-Wesley.

Encyclopedia Britannica's Editors, "William Wilberforce: British politician," *Britannica*, Published July 20, 1998, Updated August 20, 2020, https://www.britannica.com/biography/William-Wilberforce.

"Wesley to Wilberforce," Christianity Today, Accessed October 10, 2020, https://www.christianitytoday.com/history/issues/issue-2/wesley-to-wilberforce.

THE SWEEPING TEST

*"Success is to be measured not so much
by the position that one has reached
in life as by the obstacles which he has
overcome while trying to succeed."*
Booker T. Washington

1872 – Hampton Institute, Hampton, Virginia: Booker arrived at the school with fifty cents in his pocket. Exhausted and filthy after walking almost 300 miles, he was unsure whether they would take him as a student. Assistant principal Mary Mackey interviewed him and then asked him to sweep a room.

Booker meticulously swept and dusted the room three times. He passed his "sweeping test" and became a student at one of the nation's top industrial education schools for freedmen. During the three years of course work, Booker worked as the assistant janitor and was an outstanding student, graduating in the summer of 1875.

Booker was born to Jane, the cook on the James Burrough's plantation in Franklin County, Virginia. He never knew his father and wasn't sure of the year he was born, probably 1859. The twelve-by-sixteen foot cabin served as both their house and the cook shed for the white family. He slept on rags on the clay floor and got his first pair of new shoes at age six. Booker's job was carrying sacks of corn by mule to the mill to be ground into meal.

When the Civil War ended in 1865, Jane and her children were freed. They loaded their few belongings in a small wagon and traveled to Malden, West Virginia, where Jane married another former slave, Washington Ferguson. Booker joined his stepfather working in the salt furnaces nearby.

During trips to and from work, Booker passed a small school for freedmen. He convinced his stepfather to let him attend the school, with the stipulation that Booker would work at the salt furnace from 4 a.m. until 9 a.m. when school started. On the first day of class, Booker realized that most children had two names. He chose Washington for his second name because it was the best name that he knew.

In 1866, Booker became a houseboy for Viola Ruffner, the wife of a coal miner. She recognized his intelligence and integrity, and supported his desire to be educated. He worked for the Ruffners for roughly four years until 1872 when he left home and walked almost 300 miles to the Hampton Institute in Hampton, Virginia.

After graduating from the Hampton Institute, Booker returned to his old school in Malden and taught for three years before returning to Hampton to teach night classes. In 1881, the principal at Hampton was contacted by a group of white citizens from Tuskegee, Alabama, who were interested in creating an industrial education school based on the Hampton model.

Although they preferred a white principal, Booker got the job based on Armstrong's recommendation. He accepted the position site unseen. In June 1881, Booker arrived in the small community of 2,000 to start a school. He soon discovered that the group had only an idea—there was no building or land on which to build a school.

On July 4, 1881, Booker T. Washington started the Tuskegee Normal and Industrial Institute in an old church. About thirty students came on the first day. With the help of a $2,000 grant from the Alabama Legislature, the school purchased an old farmhouse and 100 acres of land. Over the years, he used his influence to raise funds to improve the facilities and grow the enrollment.

In the next two decades, Booker T. Washington became one of the most influential Black leaders in America. In 1900, he started the National Negro Business League, and his story became well known through his autobiography *Up From Slavery* the following year. He served as an advisor to Presidents Franklin Roosevelt and William Taft.

Booker T. Washington died November 14, 1915 and was buried on campus near the Tuskegee University Chapel. Today, Tuskegee University sits on 5,000 acres and has approximately 3,000 students. The school offers a broad range of programs including: business management, engineering, biomedical sciences, veterinary medicine, nursing, computer science, and education.

REFERENCES

Biography.com Editors, "Booker T. Washington," Biography.com, Last updated January 10, 2020, https://www.biography.com/activist/booker-t-washington.

Booker T. Washington, *Up from Slavery: An Autobiography,* (New York City: Doubleday).

History.com Editors, "Booker T. Washington," History.com, Updated December 13, 2019, https://www.history.com/topics/black-history/booker-t-washington.

Louis R. Harlan, "Booker T. Washington, 1856-1915," Documenting the American South, Accessed November 2, 2020, https://docsouth.unc.edu/fpn/washington/bio.

Richard Wormser, "Booker T. Washington," Jim Crow Stories, *Thirteen Media with Impact: PBS,* Accessed November 2, 2020, https://www.thirteen.org/wnet/jimcrow/stories_people_booker.

THE PEA ISLAND LIFESAVERS

*"God will not look you over for medals,
degrees, or diplomas, but for scars."*
Elbert Hubbard

June 1878 – Pea Island, North Carolina: Station No. 17, the Pea Island Life Saving Station, was created as one of eighteen stations on the Outer Banks of North Carolina. Congress established the stations to help rescue passengers and cargo in the event of a shipwreck—a common occurrence at the time. The stations were manned with a keeper, who was the commanding officer, plus six surf men and were located six miles apart along the barrier island beaches.

Stations were manned from April through November, the stormiest months on the calendar. Surf men manned towers to constantly observe the ocean and walked beach patrol between the stations around the clock. The teams used two rescue methods: they either rowed out to the wreck in a wooden surfboat or they fired a Lyle Gun, a small cannon that shot a lifeline to the ship, then rigged a pulley system to bring passengers to shore.

In 1878, 126 men were employed in the North Carolina stations. Of this number, just over a handful were Black and they were employed in the No. 6 Surf Man position as cooks.

In the spring of 1880, the station keeper and No. 1 Surf Man for the Pea Island Station were not at their post when a ship wrecked and over one hundred passengers drowned. As a result, they were fired for dereliction of duties and Richard Etheredge, a thirty-eight-year-old Civil War Veteran, was promoted to keeper. Etheredge, who had been the No. 6 Surf Man at the Body Island Station, was the first Black man to serve as a keeper in the U.S. Life Saving Service.

Etheredge had been born a slave on Roanoke Island, North Carolina, in 1842. He grew up fishing, oystering, and piloting boats on the North Carolina coast for his owner, John Etheredge. Although against the law, his owner taught him to read and write. In 1863, Richard Etheredge joined the Union Army's 36th Colored Troop. He initially served as a prison guard but was promoted to sergeant after distinguishing himself at the Battle of Richmond.

On the day that Etheredge arrived at the Pea Island Station the five white surf men quit. Six Black surf men were transferred to the station to replace them. A month later, angry that Etheredge had been promoted over whites, surf men from Station No. 16 burned the Pea Island Station to the ground. Undaunted, Etheredge supervised the rebuilding project under the protection of armed guards.

Painfully aware the standards had to be higher at Pea Island, Etheredge drilled his men with military precision. They practiced with the surfboat and Lyle Gun twice a week. He maintained a first-class crew, a meticulous logbook, and a spotless station.

At noon on October 11, 1896, keeper Etheredge wrote in his logbook "experiencing hurricane conditions." Despite the storm, the surf men maintained a vigilant watch from the tower. At 9 p.m. Theodore Meekins saw a flare to the north. The crew dispatched and pulled the Lyle Gun two miles to discover the 390-ton schooner *E.S. Newman* had run aground off the beach.

The Lyle Gun was of no use in the driving wind and rain. Etheredge asked for two volunteers to don life vests and risk their lives in order to swim to the ship with a rope. Nine times the surf men took turns swimming out through the crashing waves to bring back all nine passengers, including the captain's three-year-old son.

From 1895 to 1900, the Pea Island Lifesavers rescued passengers from six shipwrecks with one hundred percent success rate. Richard Etheredge served as the keeper at Pea Island for twenty years until his death in 1900 at age fifty-eight from pneumonia. The Pea Island Station maintained a legacy of Black surf men and remained among the best-run stations in the country until it closed in 1947.

On October 11, 1996, in Washington, D.C., one hundred years after the heroic rescue of the passengers from the *E.S. Newman*, the U.S. Coast Guard recognized descendants of Richard Etheredge and the Pea Island Lifesavers with the Coast Guard Gold Life Saving Medal, their highest award.

REFERENCES

"Captain Richard Etheridge, Keeper, USLSS," United States Coast Guard U.S. Department of Homeland Security, Accessed November 22, 2020, https://www.history.uscg.mil/Portals/1/personnel/pdf/Richard_Etheridge.pdf.

Douglas Stover, "Pea Island Life-Saving Station," National Park Service U.S. Department of Interior, May 19, 2020, https://www.nps.gov/parkhistory/online_books/caha/life_saving_hrs.pdf.

LT Connie Braesch, "Coast Guard Heroes: Richard Etheridge," Coast Guard Compass, October 27, 2010, https://coastguard.dodlive.mil/2010/10/coast-guard-heroes-richard-etheridge/.

Rescue Men: The Story of the Pea Island Lifesavers, directed by Allan R. Smith, (2010: Los Angeles, CA: Dream Quest Productions).

THE BREADLINE CHAMPION

"We shall draw from the heart of suffering itself the means of inspiration and survival."
Winston Churchill

June 13, 1935 – Madison Square Garden, New York City: More than 30,000 people packed into The Garden that evening. In living rooms across America, millions more sat glued to their radios. James J. "Jimmy" Braddock was fighting reigning heavyweight boxing champion Max Baer for the world title.

The country's heart had been moved by a man they had come to know as the "Cinderella Man." A New York sportswriter dubbed Braddock the "Cinderella Man" because of his fairy tale rise from a washed-up local boxer to the heavyweight championship, but Braddock's story was hardly one of fairy tales—it was a story of survival.

Braddock was born in 1907 on 48th Street in New York City, a couple of blocks from Madison Square Garden. His early ambition was to play football at the University of Notre Dame, but with more brawn than brains he turned to boxing. He honed his amateur boxing skills around Long Island and at age twnety-one he turned pro as a heavyweight fighter. Over the next three years, Braddock rose through the boxing ranks with a record of 44-2-2 with 21 knockouts.

Unfortunately, like millions of Americans, Braddock lost everything in the stock market crash of 1929. He knew firsthand the fear, humiliation, and hopelessness that came from standing in a breadline to feed his family. On this summer night, Braddock was a much-needed champion for the millions who huddled around their radios praying that somehow Jimmy Braddock, a ten to one underdog, could do the impossible.

Compounding his dire financial situation, in 1929 Braddock also broke his right hand in a fight and his boxing career took a nose-dive as he lost sixteen of his next twenty-two bouts. Discouraged, and fearing his career might be over, Braddock stopped training and went to work whenever he could as a longshoreman on the docks. He got an occasional boxing bout to help with the bills.

By 1933, with few boxing opportunities and work hard to find at the docks, Braddock swallowed his pride and signed up for government assistance to buy milk and bread for his three children. During that winter, his circumstances went from bad to desperate. Because he couldn't afford to pay the power bill, the electricity was turned off to the family's apartment and social services took his three children away.

By 1934, hopes and dreams were about all Braddock had left of his boxing career, but his luck was about to change. Due to a last-minute cancellation, he was given an unexpected fight with a highly regarded heavyweight boxer named Corn Griffin. No one expected Braddock to knock Griffin out in the third round, but he did. In early 1935, Braddock's fairy tale continued when he defeated Art Laskey, another contender.

In May 1935, the handlers of heavyweight champion Max Baer, thinking Braddock would be an easy pay day, handpicked him for the championship fight. Baer took Braddock lightly and hardly trained for the fight. Braddock on the other hand, trained as if his family's very lives depended on the outcome, because they did. While Baer was fighting to defend his title, Braddock was fighting for bread and milk.

When asked by a reporter if he was afraid of Baer's vicious punching ability (Baer had killed Frankie Campbell in a fight in 1930) Braddock responded, "Fighting a Max Baer, or a Bengal tiger, will be a picnic compared to what I have had to face over the last few years." Across America, Braddock was fighting for anyone who was down on their luck and for all who had ever been given up on.

The crowd came to The Garden pulling for the underdog, but they also came expecting an early round knock out by Baer. Outweighed by forty pounds, Braddock survived the first three rounds. As the crowd roared, his confidence grew. Carried by 30,000 voices, Braddock stunned the boxing world with a unanimous fifteen-round decision. On that night, Jimmy Braddock's heart was bigger than his talent. On that night, one man's courageous comeback inspired a whole country to keep fighting.

REFERENCES

Boxing News, "Max Baer vs. James Braddock," Boxing.com, June 12, 2020, http://www.boxing.com/jim_braddock_vs_max_baer.

Cinderella Man, directed by Ron Howard, (2005; New York City: Universal Pictures).

John F. McKenna (McJack), "Famous Ring Wars: Max Baer Vs Jimmy Braddock 'The Cinderella Man,'" Boxing News 24, January 8, 2012, https://www.boxingnews24.com/2012/01/famous-ring-wars-max-baer-vs-jimmy-braddock.

Wikipedia, "Cinderella Man," Last updated October 26, 2020, https://en.wikipedia.org/wiki/Cinderella_Man.

THE PRAYER MEETING

"The earnest prayer of a righteous
person has great power and
produces wonderful results."
James 5:16

Noon - Wednesday, September 23, 1857 - New York City:
Jeremiah Lanphier waited in a small room on the third
floor of the Sunday school building at the rear of the
North Dutch Reform Church. The grand old church sat
in the heart of the business district just around the corner from Wall Street. Established in 1769 by early Dutch
settlers, church construction pre-dated the Revolutionary War by six years.

Forty-eight-year-old Jeremiah Calvin Lanphier,
originally from Coxsackie, New York, had run a small
mercantile business in the city for nearly twenty years
before putting his business on hold. In an effort to save
its dwindling congregation, the church appointed Lanphier to become a missionary to businessmen of New
York City. His task had been a bold, unique undertak-

ing. After uttering a simple prayer, "Lord, what would you have me to do?" he felt lead to start a weekly prayer meeting for businessmen.

Lanphier published handbills to advertise the noon meeting and placed them in local businesses. The day of the event arrived, and when no one showed by 12:10 p.m., he began pacing the floor. At twenty minutes past the hour, he had begun to wonder about the merit of his idea. At 12:35 p.m., just as he was thinking of leaving, he heard someone coming up the stairs.

Six businessmen attended Lanphier's first prayer meeting. Twenty men joined the group the second week and by the third week the number doubled to forty. Encouraged by the response, Lanphier moved the prayer meeting to a daily noon event.

In the summer of 1857, a recession plagued New York City. On August 30, the Ohio Life Insurance Company and its bank failed. A week later the New Haven Railroad failed. By the time Lanphier began his first prayer meeting in September, twenty-nine banks had failed in New York City. On October 14, the Bank of New York, the oldest and strongest bank in the city, failed along with fourteen other banks, triggering the Financial Crisis of 1857. The Bond Market failed and widespread panic diffused from New York City to the rest of America and Europe.

Spurred by the financial crisis, Lanphier's prayer meeting numbers grew exponentially. Within a few months, the North Dutch Church participants over-flowed to the John Street Methodist Church near Broadway. Soon, the Metropolitan Theater on Chambers Street was packed at noon each day with up to 2,000 people praying. Six months after the initial prayer meeting, an estimated 10,000 people were praying across New York City as many businesses shut down during the noon hour so their employees could attend.

Over the course of a year, the mid-day prayer meetings spread to Boston, Chicago, Philadelphia, and Washington D.C.. At a Chicago meeting, a twenty-one-year-old shoe salesman named Dwight L. Moody felt a call to Christian service. He later became one of the greatest evangelists in American history.

The period between 1857 and 1859 was considered the greatest awakening of human hearts in the history of America. An estimated one million lives were changed at noon prayer meetings across the country. Because the U.S. population was only 30 million people, roughly a tenth of today's population, that number equates to 10 million people today.

The movement started with one man on his knees in the third-floor lecture room of the North Dutch Reformed Church on Fulton Street in New York City. A simple prayer, a willing heart, and an act of obedience led to a nationwide revival.

REFERENCES

Dan Graves, "Jeremy Lanphier Led Prayer Revival," Christianity.com, Last updated June 2007, https://www.christianity.com/church/church-history/timeline/1801-1900/jeremy-lanphier-led-prayer-revival-11630507.

"Revival Born in Prayer Meeting," Knowing & Doing, Originally published in the Fall 2004 edition of Knowing & Doing, Accessed November 22, 2020, https://www.cslewisinstitute.org/webfm_send/577.

Wilbur M. Smith, "The Fulton Street Prayer Meeting and the Great Revival," The Sunday School Times, June 1, 1957.

UNCHARTERED WATERS

---

*"Beware in your prayer above everything,
of limiting God. Expect the unexpected,
above all that we can ask or think."*
A.B. Simpson

*Monday, January 19, 2015 – St. Joseph Hospital, Lake
St. Louis, Missouri:* John Smith had been dead for more
than thirty minutes when he arrived at the emergency room. The paramedics had done all they could do.
Dr. Kent Stutterer and his emergency team worked on
the fourteen-year-old drowning victim for an additional twenty minutes, but there was still no heartbeat. Dr.
Stutterer called the waiting room and asked John's parents to come back to his room.

Racing to the hospital after getting the call about
the accident, John's mother, Joyce, a woman of faith, had
pleaded with God not to take her son. When she got the
news from Dr. Stutterer, she screamed, "No! No! Lord,
please, please don't take John! I believe you are a God
who can do miracles!" God heard a desperate mother's

cry—the heart monitor started beeping. Despite having been dead for almost an hour, John's heart was beating.

When Brian and Joyce Smith's biological sons were ages twenty-eight and thirty, they decided to adopt a child. In November 2000, they flew to Guatemala to adopt nine-month-old John. He grew up to love basketball and was the point guard and star of his eighth-grade team. On the Martin Luther King holiday weekend in January 2015, he spent the night with a fellow basketball player, Josh Riegers.

Unusually cold weather had caused the seventy acre lake in Josh's neighborhood to freeze and on Monday morning the boys couldn't resist walking across the ice. When they were 150 feet from shore, the ice cracked and the boys fell into the lake.

Ron Wilson, the neighborhood association manager, saw the boys fall through the ice and called 911. It was 11:33 a.m. Fire department paramedics arrived a few minutes later to find Josh clinging to the ice, but no sign of John. Donning thermal gear and using long poles with hooks, they miraculously fished John's lifeless body out of the lake at 11:51 a.m.

After being stabilized, John was transferred to Cardinal Glennon Children's Medical Center in St. Louis forty miles away. Dr. Jeremy Garrett, a drowning specialist, met the transport there. After reading the report, Dr. Garrett spoke with the family and told them, "Mr. and Mrs. Smith, John has a one percent chance of survival.

If he somehow survives, he will never regain consciousness. His heart is beating, but he has no brain function."

"Stop speaking negative words over John!" Joyce shouted. "I've been told that you are the best, so here is what I want you to do. Do your best in what you know to do, and my God will do the rest." Although shocked, the doctor complied.

On Tuesday morning, John squeezed Joyce's hand when she spoke to him, but doctors said it was an involuntary reflex. On Wednesday, he opened his eyes and turned his head. The nurse called the doctor and reported "John's awake!" When Dr. Garrett arrived, John opened his eyes and gave a thumbs up when the doctor asked if he liked basketball. Dr. Garrett motioned Joyce into the hallway and shrugged, "This really isn't possible, but God…"

John remained on a ventilator and feeding tube. By Thursday, Garrett and his team were bringing specific prayer requests to Joyce and her band of prayer warriors gathered in the hospital lobby. Ten days after the accident, John walked out of the hospital. He returned to school a month later.

In May 2019, John graduated from Living Word Christian School. He attends North Central University, a Christian college in Minneapolis, Minnesota. After college John plans to enter the ministry. "I am glad God chose to save me," John says. "God has a plan for my life, just like he has a plan for everybody. He gave me a story to share with others."

REFERENCES

Breakthrough: The Story. The People, www.breakthroughmovie.com.

Dewayne Hamby, "Meet the Real People Behind the 'Breakthrough' Miracle Story," Charisma News, April 18, 2019, https://www.charismanews.com/culture/76006-meet-the-real-people-behind-the-breakthrough-miracle-story.

Joyce Smith and Ginger Kolbaba, *Breakthrough: The Miraculous True Story of a Mother's Faith and Her Child's Resurrection*, (Nashville: Faith Words Publishing, 2019).

FLYING IS FOR ANGELS

*"I have learned to use the word impossible
with the greatest of caution."*
Werner von Braun

Early 1870s – Hartsville College, Hartsville, Indiana: The college president opened the United Brethren Churches conference with the comment, "We live in an exciting age, the age of inventions." The United Brethren bishop interrupted him, "What kinds of inventions?"

The college president responded, "Why, for example, I believe that one day we will be able to fly through the air like birds." The bishop scolded him, "That is heresy, absolute heresy! The Bible says that flight is reserved for the angels. We will have no such talk at this conference." At the end of the conference, Bishop Milton Wright returned home to his wife and two young sons in Dayton, Ohio.

Wilbur Wright, the second son of Milton and Susan Wright, was born in 1867. Four years later, his brother Orville was born. When they were ages seven and eleven, Bishop Wright bought the boys a fluttering helicopter-like toy made of cork with a rubber band-driven propeller. They played with the toy until it broke, then they built one. The toy sparked in Wilbur and Orville a lifelong fascination in flying.

Both boys attended high school, but neither graduated. In 1889, the brothers designed and built a small printing press and began publishing a daily newspaper. In 1892, capitalizing on the national bicycle craze, they opened a small bicycle repair shop in Dayton. Four years later, the brothers began building their own bicycle which they called the Wright Flyer.

In 1896, Chicago aviation pioneer Octave Chanute successfully tested gliders on the shores of Lake Michigan. His success convinced the brothers that flight was possible. They read every article they could find about aviation. They also contacted the National Weather Service which recommended Kitty Hawk, North Carolina, as an ideal location for testing gliders due to its prevailing winds and open beaches.

In 1900, using proceeds from their bicycle shop, Wilbur and Orville traveled by train to Kitty Hawk. They began by flying large double-winged kites and then progressed to unmanned gliders. In the summer of 1901, they built gliders with larger wingspans and made dozens of manned glider flights traveling distances up to 400 feet.

This success whetted their appetite to build a powered flying machine. In 1903, the brothers built the Wright Flyer I out of spruce wood, woven fabric wings, and a specially-designed engine with a wooden propeller they copied from a boat motor.

Despite repeated failures, and the fact that what they were trying to do was considered impossible, the two bicycle mechanics kept trying. They were so confident of their success they had hired a photographer. On the morning of December 17, 1903, he captured a picture when their "heavier-than-air flying machine" lifted off the rails for the first time. Orville flew 120 feet in twelve seconds. Later that day, Wilbur flew for fifty-nine seconds.

On that same day, they sent a telegram to their father and sister, Katherine, in Dayton. It read, "Success. Four flights today. First flight 12 seconds. Longest 59 seconds. Home for Christmas." Katherine placed a message in the Dayton newspaper. Although her brothers had just revolutionized travel on planet earth, the local headlines read, "Popular local bicycle mechanics will be home for the holidays."

The brothers continued to improve their flying machines, and on May 25, 1910, their eighty-one-year-old father accompanied them to an airfield eight miles outside of Dayton. The brothers wanted to demonstrate their latest design, an airplane with wheels; no longer would they rely on a wooden rail to launch their planes.

Over the years, Milton Wright had reconsidered his position on flying and had become his sons' biggest fan. Late in the afternoon, Orville took Milton for his first flight. For seven minutes, they flew at an altitude of 350 feet. Concerned about his father's reaction, Orville was thrilled when Milton leaned close to his ear and shouted over the engine noise, "Higher, Orville, higher!"

REFERENCES

History.com Editors, "Wright Brothers," History.com, June 6, 2019, https://www.history.com/topics/inventions/wright-brothers.

"The Wright Stories," Accessed November 1, 2020, www.wrightstories.com.

"Wright Brothers Aeroplane Company: A Virtual Museum of Pioneer Aviation," Accessed November 1, 2020, www.wright-brothers.org.

"Wright Brothers," Smithsonian National Air and Space Museum, Accessed November 1, 2020, https://airandspace.si.edu/learn/highlighted-topics/wright-brothers.

THE LADY BEHIND THE BRIDGE

"I determined never to stop until I had come to the end and achieved my purpose."
David Livingstone

May 24, 1883 – Brooklyn Bridge, New York City: With tears in his eyes, Washington Roebling watched through his telescope as his wife Emily rode in a carriage across the newly completed Brooklyn Bridge. On her lap was a rooster, a symbol of victory.

In recognition of her accomplishments on the bridge project, New York City honored Emily by allowing her to be the first person to cross the bridge. At nearly 1,600 feet long, it was the world's longest suspension bridge. Its twin towers were taller than any building in the world and connected Brooklyn to Manhattan.

Emily Warren was born in Cold Springs, New York in September 1843. She was educated at the Georgetown Visitation Convent in Washington, D.C., the nation's second oldest girl's school. In January 1865, she married

Washington Roebling, a civil engineer and bridge builder. Washington's father, John Roebling, was the most famous bridge builder in the country, having built suspension bridges in Pittsburgh, Cincinnati, and Niagara Falls.

In 1869, New York City officials approved John Roebling's long-time dream of building a suspension bridge across the East River. However, two weeks later, John died of tetanus leaving thirty-two-year-old Washington to replace his father as chief engineer on one of the most significant civil engineering projects of the century.

Washington's first challenge was to construct two massive towers, one on each side of the river, to string the hundreds of steel cables that would support the bridge. He built pneumatic caissons—large, air-locked, enclosed wooden chambers that allowed men to work underwater—to pour the tower foundations on the river bottom. Washington spent so much time down in the caissons that he developed compression sickness and by 1872 he was partially paralyzed and entirely bedridden for the rest of his life.

In order for Washington to continue his role as chief engineer, the Roeblings bought a house in Brooklyn Heights within walking distance of the bridge. With the aid of a telescope, Washington could watch bridge construction from his bedroom window.

With Washington confined to the house, each night he wrote the next day's construction plan and each morning, and often several times a day, Emily walked to the bridge to cover the instructions with the crews. Washington began to tutor Emily in the fundamentals of suspension bridge engineering and construction. He taught her calculus, strength of materials, stress analysis, steel cable construction, and all facets of project management.

Emily assumed most of Washington's chief engineering duties, keeping detailed records and handling everything from the daily supervision of bridge activities to project management. In an era when many considered a woman's brain incapable of understanding complex engineering principals, the thought of a woman being responsible for building the biggest bridge in the world was too ridiculous for some New Yorkers to contemplate. Newspapers frequently questioned Emily's ability to manage such a massive undertaking.

Late in the project, when bridge construction faced delays and cost overruns, there was a growing sentiment among New York public officials and city engineers to replace Washington Roebling as the chief engineer. Emily met with elected officials, passionately presented Washington's case, and convinced them to allow him to finish the job.

The Brooklyn Bridge was finally completed in May 1883, ten years after its projected completion date and fourteen years after the project began. U.S. President Chester A. Arthur and an estimated 50,000 people attended the bridge dedication. Later that day, President

Arthur attended a reception at the Roebling home to thank them for their tenacity and teamwork in completing John Roebling's dream.

REFERENCES

"Emily Warren Roebling," American Society of Civil Engineers, Accessed November 23, 2020, https://www.asce.org/templates/person-bio-detail.aspx-?id=11203.

Encyclopedia Britannica Editors, "Emily Warren Roebling," Britannica, Last updated September 19, 2020, https://www.britannica.com/biography/Emily-Warren-Roebling.

Jessica Li, "Emily Roebling: The Engineer Behind the Bridge," ScientistA, January 16, 2015, http://www.scientistafoundation.com/scientista-spotlights/emily-roebling-the-engineer-behind-the-brooklyn-bridge.

"Roebling Museum," Accessed November 23, 2020, www.roeblingmuseum.org.

GETTING FIRED AND A
NATIONAL CHAMPIONSHIP

*"If I had not gotten fired from my job
as Head Football Coach at Arkansas,
I never would have lived my dream of
coaching football at Notre Dame and
winning the National Championship."*
Lou Holtz

Sunday, December 18, 1983 – Fayetteville, Arkansas:
Arkansas Head Football Coach Lou Holtz had just
returned from church when Athletic Director Franks
Broyles called and asked him to come by his office.
When Holtz arrived, Broyles got right to the point,
"Lou, I want you to resign." Holtz thought he was jok-
ing, but Broyles was dead serious. "Why?" Holtz asked.
"I just think it is best for the program," Broyles replied.
The news hit Holtz like a ton of bricks.

Holtz and his wife Beth had hoped that Arkansas
would be their last stop and they had talked about retiring in Fayetteville. He had the best win-loss record (60-
21) in University of Arkansas history, had the second best
win-loss record ever in the Southwest Conference, and
during his tenure Arkansas had received seven consecu-

tive postseason bowl invitations. Holtz didn't think that he deserved to be fired. He was angry and hurt.

The following day Harvey Mackey, a successful businessman, New York Times best-selling author, and personal friend gave Holtz a call. Mackey, who was a University of Minnesota alumnus, was helping the athletic director fill the head coach position. He wanted Holtz to come to Minnesota. As far as Holtz was concerned, Minneapolis was the North Pole. Beth encouraged him to stay positive instead of moping around and feeling bitter, so he followed her advice and packed for a trip to Minnesota.

It was snowing during the drive to the airport to catch their flight and Holtz threatened to go back home. "No," Beth advised, "we're more than halfway to the airport and the snow is easing up. Plus, there's nothing waiting for us back in Fayetteville." Despite temperatures in the single digits and lots of snow on the ground, Holtz liked the people and the program at Minnesota.

When he and Beth prayed about the decision in their hotel room, Holtz had a sense of peace about the offer and he got an idea. He asked the University of Minnesota for a Notre Dame clause—if in the future Notre Dame offered Holtz a job, and if Minnesota were bowl eligible, he could terminate his contract and accept the position.

Holtz, a devout Catholic, had grown up in Ohio with a dream of coaching football at Notre Dame. The sisters of Notre Dame taught him in high school, and he marched to the Notre Dame fight song at recess, lunch, and afternoon dismissal.

The Minnesota athletic director initially balked at Holtz's request. But Holtz was the fifth coach offered the job and after two days the athletic director agreed to the clause. In 1984, Holtz became the head coach at the University of Minnesota and won four games. The following season his team went 6-5 and was invited to the Independence Bowl in Shreveport, Louisiana. Holtz got a call a week after the bowl that began, "Lou Holtz, this is Father Joyce from Notre Dame…"

On January 2, 1989, in Sun Devil Stadium, Tempe, Arizona, Coach Lou Holtz's No. 1 ranked Fighting Irish beat No. 3 West Virginia to go 13-0 for the season and win the college football national championship.

According to Holtz in an interview on his journey, "Things are not always going to go the way you would like them to go and it is important to maintain a good attitude and don't ever lose sight of your dreams. If I had been able to see the future and known what would happen five years later," Holtz smiled, "I might have hugged Frank Broyles neck when he asked for my resignation. You never know when bad things are intended to lead you in a good direction."

REFERENCES

Associated Press, "Lou Holtz Resigns as Coach at Arkansas," *Associated Press,* New York Times (New York City, NY), Dec. 19, 1983.

Lou Holtz, *Wins, Losses, and Lessons: An Autobiography*, (New York City: Harper Collins Publishers, 2006), 173-195.

The City Wire Staff Writer, "Lou Holtz shares laughs, memories about Razorbacks," Talk Business & Politics, Published September 23, 2013, https://talkbusiness.net/2013/09/lou-holtz-shares-laughs-memories-about-the-razorbacks.

MARIANNE'S PRAYER

*"I never prayed sincerely and earnestly
for anything but it came at sometime;
no matter at how distant a day,
somehow, in some shape, probably the
least I would have devised, it came."*
Adoniram Judson

June 1872 – New Court Congregational Church, London:
After Dwight L. Moody preached at the church on a Sunday morning, a young woman hurried home and told her bed-ridden sister, "Mr. Moody from America preached at our church this morning." Marianne Adlard shouted, "I know what that means, God has heard my prayers!"

When Mr. Moody had preached in the Sunday morning service, a less than enthusiastic crowd made him doubt why he had preached. But what began when he preached on Sunday night in the little church would become the greatest revival in Great Britain since John Wesley preached 130 years earlier.

Marianne, bedridden for years, never attended church. She was deeply burdened for friends and family, and she prayed daily for a revival. But she didn't just pray for revival, she prayed that Dwight L. Moody would come from Chicago to preach a revival at her church.

Moody had visited England five years earlier and Marianne had read about his visit. Since then, she couldn't get him off her mind. She had clipped the newspaper article and kept it under her pillow. She felt moved to ask God to send Mr. Moody to New Court Congregational Church—the idea pressed on her.

Dwight Lyman Moody was born in Northfield, Massachusetts in 1837. When he was seventeen, he began work in his uncle's shoe store in Boston and at age eighteen, he moved to Chicago with a dream to make his fortune selling shoes. At age twenty-one, Moody started a Sunday class for young men. Encouraged by the quick growth of the class, and against the strong advice of close friends, in February of 1864, Moody founded the Illinois Street Church and became the first pastor.

Illinois Street Church would later become the great Moody Bible Church and the Moody Bible Institute. As Moody was concluding his sermon on Sunday, October 8, 1871, the fire bells began to ring. He lost everything that he had built later that afternoon in the Great Chicago Fire. He had believed that God wanted him to start a church, but now he wasn't sure… maybe his friends had been right.

In the spring of 1872, needing guidance and direction, Moody left his wife Emma and two children in Chicago and traveled to England for a spiritual sabbatical. He would not preach but would just sit at the feet of some of England's greatest preachers—men like Charles Spurgeon and George Mueller. Moody's close friends urged him to give up his absurd idea, but after much prayer and deliberation Moody arrived in London in June 1872.

Shortly after arriving, Moody discretely slipped into a mid-week prayer service in the Central Criminal Court Building. Having recognized Moody from his previous visit to London, Pastor John Lessey begged him to preach at his North Court Congregational Church the following Sunday. Moody was reluctant; he had not come to England to preach, but he finally agreed.

On that Sunday night when Moody preached at North Court "the very atmosphere was charged with the Spirit of God." When he gave the altar call, almost everyone in the church stood up. Thinking the people had misunderstood, Moody had everyone sit back down. After explaining the altar call a second time, almost 400 people came to the altar.

Word spread about the Sunday night service at North Court and hundreds more came to the church the following week. Moody preached there for two weeks before being invited to Chelsea Chapel. His preaching had similar results. Moody preached all across England before returning to Chicago in September.

In 1873, Moody returned to England with his family and for two years he led revivals in England, Scotland,

Ireland, and Wales. At times, as many as 15,000 people crowded into the great halls to hear him preach.

Dwight L. Moody is estimated to have preached to 100 million people before his death in 1899. The former shoe salesman is one of the greatest evangelists of the nineteenth century. And it began with a fire-ravaged church in Chicago and the faithful prayers of Marianne Adlard.

REFERENCES

"About D. L. Moody," Moody Center, Accessed November 22, 2020, https://moodycenter.org/about-d-l-moody.

David Maas, "The Life and Times of D.L. Moody," Christian History: Christianity Today, Accessed November 22, 2020, https://www.christianitytoday.com/history/issues/issue-25/life-times-of-d-l-moody.

Henry and Richard Blackaby, *Fresh Encounter—God's Pattern for Spiritual Awakening*, (2009: Nashville, B & H Publishing), pp. 176-77.

"Meet Dwight," Moody Bible Institute, Accessed November 22, 2020, https://www.moody.edu/about/our-bold-legacy/d-l-moody.

NO REGRETS

"You are never too old to set another goal or dream a new dream."
Les Brown

Early Spring, 1999 – Big Lake, Texas: Coach Jim Morris' baseball team wasn't very good. The Reagan County Owls had won one game in each of the past three seasons. They expected to lose. Morris urged them to chase a dream—to win the district championship—something the high school had never done.

During a pep talk after practice, a player stopped Morris mid-sentence, "What about you coach? Why are you telling us to chase our dreams, if you are not willing to do it yourself?" The thirty-five-year-old coach had once dreamed of pitching in the big leagues. He pitched in the minors for four seasons before injuries ended his career. Morris made a promise to his players: If the team won the district, he would try out.

Jim Morris was born in Brownswood, Texas, in January 1964. A great baseball and football player, Morris was a first-round draft choice of the New York Yankees in 1982, but he turned them down. He wanted to get a college education first. Morris accepted a baseball scholarship to Angelo State University one hundred miles from home.

Two years later, Morris was drafted again. This time by the Milwaukee Brewers, and this time he signed a contract. He pitched four seasons in their Class A minor league system but was plagued with injuries. After his fourth arm surgery, Morris called it quits, completed his degree at Angelo State, and became a high school baseball coach.

Morris assumed his bet with his players was safe. He was confident his dream was dead because he was not confident about a district championship. However, the team made the playoffs. In the district championship game, they scored four runs in the last inning to win. As Morris drove the excited team bus back to their school, his players reminded him of their deal.

A month after the championship, in June 1999, Morris kept his promise. He expected to embarrass himself by trying out, but he drove two hours to a Tampa Bay Devil Rays tryout camp. His wife had to work that day and, unbeknownst to her, Morris tooktheir three young children with him. The scouts laughed when he arrived pushing the youngest child in a stroller.

Morris waited three hours in 100-degree heat and was the last player to try out. Tired of jokes about his age, he almost left, but didn't because of the promise he made to his team. When Morris threw the first pitch, he noticed a scout shake his radar gun. Morris wondered to himself, *did I not even throw hard enough to register a velocity?* It got quiet when the big lefty threw ten straight pitches at ninety-eight miles per hour.

That day when he got home, Morris had an interesting conversation with his wife Lorri about the kids and his day, and he got several calls from scouts that night. Would he come back in two days and pitch again? They wanted to verify his velocity. He would, he did, and later that week, Morris signed a contract with Tampa Bay.

Three months later, and eleven years after his last minor league game, on September 18, 1999, in front of his family and his high school team, Jim Morris made his major league debut on the mound for the Tampa Bay Devil Rays against the Texas Rangers in Arlington, Texas. He struck out the first batter he faced. Lorri cried.

Jim Morris became the oldest player in thirty years to make the major leagues, a thirty-five-year-old chemistry teacher with an old dream and a ninety-eight-mile-hour fastball. He was a relief pitcher for two seasons with Tampa Bay and the Los Angeles Dodgers. Although he only pitched in twenty-one games, Jim Morris fulfilled a promise and a dream.

REFERENCES

Goalcast, "The Unbelievable True Story of Baseball's Oldest Rookie/Jim Morris Motivational Speech/ Goalcast," Youtube video, 8:12, April 17, 2018, https://www.youtube.com/watch?v=TmOUAcGW_1E.

Jim Morris, "Jim Morris Biography," Web Solutions LLC., Accessed November 5, 2020, https://sports.jrank.org/pages/3337/Morris-Jim.html.

"Jim 'The Rookie' Morris," Facts, Video, Jim "The Rookie" Morris, Accessed November 5, 2020, https://www.jimtherookiemorris.com/.

Tyler O'Shea, "Jim "The Rookie" Morris on Living Your Dreams," Joker Magazine, June 20, 2019, www.jokermagazine.com.

Wikipedia, "Jim Morris," Last modified August 14, 2020, https://en.wikipedia.org/wiki/Jim_Morris.

OPERATION YELLOW RIBBON

"Try to be a rainbow in someone's cloud."
Maya Angelo

3 p.m., Monday, September 11, 2001 – Gander, Newfoundland: American Airlines Flight 49 was en route from Paris to Dallas when Captain Beverly Bass called for the head flight attendant. Bass handed her a printed message from the American Airlines office in Dallas. It read, "All airways over the Continental United States are closed to commercial air traffic. Make an emergency landing in Gander, Newfoundland."

American Airlines Flight 49 detoured 400 miles to the airport in Gander. It was the thirty-sixth commercial plane to land there that day. The confused passengers were told the plane had mechanical problems and it would be twenty-eight hours before they would leave the plane and discover the real story.

At 11 a.m. that morning Gander Mayor Claude Elliott had gotten a call for help when the first plane, Virgin Air Flight 75 with 337 passengers en route from London to Orlando, landed at the town's airport. Elliott notified the local Red Cross and Salvation Army then opened an emergency operation at the town hall. The town of Gander had only 10,000 residents, but its World War II era airport featured two 10,000-foot runways—the longest runways between Europe and North America.

By late afternoon, thirty-eight commercial planes bound for the U.S. from Europe were on the ground in Gander. A total of 6,132 passengers from 40 countries and 463 crewmembers awaited instructions. The first priority was for a local pharmacy to bring Nicorette gum and nicotine patches.

Elliott called churches, schools, fire stations, the Lions Club, and the Knights of Columbus asking for assistance and then requested the small towns within thirty miles set up emergency shelters. Gander's 550 hotel rooms would be used for the flight crews. At 4:30 p.m. passengers from Virgin Air Flight 75, the first plane to land, cleared customs and were met by 200 volunteers. Passengers were only allowed to bring carry-on luggage with them.

School bus drivers, who were on strike, put down their picket signs and drove passengers to shelters. At 8:30 p.m. the 400 passengers on Lufthansa Airlines Flight 430 cleared customs and were taken to a high school where they received food, toiletries, and bedding. Passengers from Continental Flight 23 were bussed fifteen miles to a church in the town of Appleton, population 700. A small Baptist church took forty refugees from Moldova off Delta Flight 141 who were headed to New York from Brussels.

Every business in town joined in the relief effort. The two grocery stores went to twenty-four-hour service. Newtel, the local phone company set up phones in their building so passengers could make free calls. Local drug stores made calls to a dozen countries to get medical information to fill prescriptions. The nine dogs, ten cats, and two monkeys on board the planes were taken to an emergency animal shelter in an airport hangar.

The Salvation Army was responsible for gathering supplies. People donated food, sheets, blankets, and old clothes. Pharmacies donated toiletries, including 4,000 toothbrushes. More than 200 people opened their homes so the "plane people" could shower.

Finally, on Friday, September 15, 2001, the planes began to leave. On Sunday afternoon the final flight, Delta Flight 141, was re-routed from New York to Atlanta. The hospitality of the people in Gander and surrounding communities during Operation Yellow Ribbon had been overwhelming.

Residents refused to accept money for their efforts, but visitors left $60,000 in the town donation box. Later, visitors established a million-dollar trust for scholarships for local students. The president of the Rockefeller Foundation, who stayed at one of the schools, was so impressed he agreed to buy all new computers for the schools.

In September 2011, on the tenth anniversary of the 9/11 tragedy, many of the passengers returned to Gander, including Captain Beverly Bass and her family. While they would eventually forget some of the horrific details of that event, they would never forget the love and kindness shown to total strangers by the people of Gander.

REFERENCES

Jim DeFede, *The Day the World Came to Town*, (New York City: Harper Collins, 2002).

Katherine Lackey, "An oasis of kindness on 9/11: This town welcomed 6,700 strangers amid terror attack," *USA Today*, September 8, 2017, https://www.usatoday.com/story/news/nation/2017/09/08/gander-newfoundland-september-11-terror-attacks-kindess-come-from-away/631329001.

Michael Schulman, "Stuck in Gander, Newfoundland," *The New Yorker,* March 27, 2017, https://www.newyorker.com/magazine/2017/03/27/stuck-in-gander-newfoundland.

MIRACLE ON THE RIVER KWAI

*"Faith could not save us from the miserable
prison camp, but it could take us through it."*
Ernest Gordon

May 1943 – Chungkai Prison Camp – Thailand: Scottish
Commander Ernest Gordon lay dying in the infamous
Japanese prison camp in a Thailand jungle on the bank
of the Kwai River. He had been placed on the ground
next to several prisoners of war, and a couple of corpses,
in the hospital/morgue known as the "Death House."

Gordon had penned a final letter to his parents telling them that he loved them. Then after cursing God
and the Japanese, he waited for death. It would be a welcomed escape from the hell he had experienced since
being captured fifteen months before.

Ernest Gordon was born in Greenock, Scotland,
in 1917. During World War II he became a company
commander with the 93rd Battalion of the Argyll and
Sutherland Highlanders. In 1942, at the Battle of Sin-

gapore, the Japanese captured him. Gordon, along with other prisoners of war, was marched into the jungles of Thailand and forced to build the notorious Burma/Thailand railroad.

On May 31, two fellow POW's from Gordon's unit brought their captain a rice ball trimmed with a banana in celebration of his twenty-seventh birthday. They were shocked by his condition. The next day his buddies, Dusty Miller and Dinty Moore, both Christians, arranged to get Gordon out of the hospital and carried him to a makeshift bamboo hut they had built.

After watching hundreds die from starvation, torture, and disease, Gordon had accepted his fate and wanted to be left alone to die. But each night, after being forced to work from sunrise until dark on the railroad, the two men shared their meager rations with Gordon. Miller patiently cleaned the infected boils on Gordon's bony legs and back and picked the lice from his body.

Gordon struggled to understand why two men who were starving would willingly share their rations with a dying man. Despite his bitterness toward them, Miller and Moore came each night with food and tattered pages from a Bible. Another POW gave a guard his watch in exchange for medicine for Gordon. Slowly, Gordon realized the men had found the answer he needed. Their love freed him from a prison of hatred, hopelessness, and despair and gave him new faith and a desire to live.

In the Chungkai camp, there was no church, no chaplain, and no religious services. Because of his leadership position and college degree, once Gordon's condition improved, he was asked to lead a Bible study on the edge of the camp. What began with a single verse shared with a dozen POW's grew to influence hundreds of men. Men stopped stealing and fighting over rations and began sharing their food. Hatred of the Japanese guards was replaced with forgiveness.

Gordon survived the war and when it ended, he returned to Scotland. He earned degrees at the University of London and Hartford Theological Seminary in Connecticut. In 1950, he was ordained by the Church of Scotland and came to Long Island, New York, to pastor churches in Amagansett and Montauk. In 1954, Gordon became the Presbyterian chaplain at Princeton University and later dean of the chapel. He served at Princeton for twenty-six years until his retirement in 1981.

After his retirement, Gordon moved to Washington, D.C. to be president of Christian Rescue Effort for the Emancipation of Dissidents, an organization that helped free prisoners from eastern European countries. He chronicled his three-year POW experience in the powerful memoir *Through the Valley of the Kwai*.

An estimated 60,000 allied POW's plus 240,000 Asians workers were forced to build the 250-mile railroad from Thailand to Burma—a five-year project that was completed in twelve months. Approximately 13,000

POW's and 80,000 civilians died from the brutal conditions and were buried along the railroad.

Dinty Moore died when his prisoner transport ship was torpedoed on the way back to Japan at the end of the war. Dusty Miller escaped from Chungkai but was later captured and killed by the Japanese two weeks before the war ended. Ernest Gordon died February 16, 2002, at the age of eighty-five.

REFERENCES

David Stout, "No Headline," New York Times, January 20, 2002, https://www.ny-times.com/2002/01/20/nyregion/no-headline-223891.

"Ernest Gordon, Longtime Dean of Chapel Dies," Princeton University Office of Communications, January 21, 2002, https://pr.princeton.edu/news/02/q1/0121-gordon.

Ernest Gordon, *To End All Wars: A True Story About the Will to Survive and the Will to Forgive,* 2013: New York City, HarperCollins Publishing).

"Through the valley of death He was driven beyond exhaustion working on the railway over the Kwai but lived to become a symbol of hope for other prisoners. Now at 85, Ernest Gordon reveals how he has made peace with the past," The Herald, August 17, 2001, https://www.heraldscotland.com/news/12172990.through-the-valley-of-death-he-was-driven-beyond-exhaustion-working-on-the-railway-over-the-kwai-but-lived-to-become-a-symbol-of-hope-for-other-prisoners-now-at-85-ernest-gordon-reveals-how-he-has-made-peace-with-the-past.

MOVER OF MOUNTAINS

"The question is not how much of my money am I going to give to God, but how much of God's money am I going to keep."
R.G. LeTourneau

1902 – Portland, Oregon: Bobbie LeTourneau's father told him, "Okay, you're determined to amount to nothing, so I'm going to let you quit school." He found his fourteen-year-old seventh grader a job as an iron molder apprentice at the East Portland Iron Works hoping that after a couple of days of the hot, backbreaking work, Bobbie would return to school, but Bobbie loved the work.

When the ironworks burned three years later, Bobbie found a job in a San Francisco foundry and became a journeyman iron molder. During the next twelve years, he got saved, got married, lost a child, and was fired several times from a string of jobs including being a: logger, construction worker, brick mason, and auto mechanic to name a few. He started out with nothing and by his late 30s he still had most of it.

In the fall of 1920, Bobbie discovered his destiny. Ironically it happened when his auto repair shop failed and his brother hired him to level forty acres of land. When Bobbie drove a tractor for the first time, he fell in love with moving dirt. He borrowed $500 to buy a used tractor, rent a scraper blade, and he went to work in the dirt moving business.

On September 19, 1921, in Stockton, California, Bobbie founded the R.G. LeTourneau Company and became known by those initials. He built a major highway between Stockton and Oakland, California, and later connected the Boulder Highway to the Hoover Dam. Over the years, the company stopped contracting and focused on building earth-moving equipment with factories in California, Illinois, Georgia, Mississippi, and Louisiana.

On June 6, 1944, when the Allied troops stormed the beaches of Normandy, France, in the largest invasion in world history, they did so with the help of machines and equipment built by the R.G. LeTourneau Company. Letourneau's machines represented seventy percent of the earth-moving equipment and engineering vehicles used in World War II.

Nobody ever told LeTourneau that a machine could not be built to handle a big job. His motto was "No big problems, just little machines," and he delighted in engineering and designing bigger and better machines. Letourneau received almost 300 patents during his lifetime. He built the first bulldozers, the first mobile scraper pans, the first log hauling machines, and the first offshore oil rigs in the Gulf of Mexico. At age seventy, LeTourneau built a rubber-tired dirt hauler that could move 150 tons of dirt, which was 1,000 times more than his first rental scraper.

LeTourneau based his company on Christian principals. He began by tithing ten percent to his church and never required his employees to work on Sunday. God blessed the business. As the company grew, so did Letourneau's giving. LeTourneau and his wife established the Letourneau Foundation and directed an increasing amount of the business profits there until ninety percent of the profits went into the foundation, and he and his family lived on ten percent.

The LeTourneau Foundation donated hundreds of millions of dollars to charities and projects around the world including funds to build hospitals, churches, and schools in Africa, South America, and Haiti. The foundation also established Letourneau University, an interdenominational liberal arts university in Longview, Texas. Today, the university has 3,000 students from all 50 states and 30 different countries.

Before his death in 1969 at age eighty-one, R.G. LeTourneau frequently shared his story of how God richly blessed an auto mechanic with a sixth-grade education. His talks usually began with "I am just a mechanic, who has been blessed by God. I shovel it out, and God shovels it back, but He has a bigger shovel."

REFERENCES

Norman V. Kelly, "R.G. LeTourneau: God's Businessman," Peoria Magazine, January 2011, https://www.peoriamagazines.com/ibi/2011/jan/rg-letourneau.

"R.G. LeTourneau – Earthmoving Innovator," Giants for God, Accessed November 22, 2020, http://www.giantsforgod.com/rg-letourneau.

R.G. LeTourneau, *Mover of Men and Mountains: The Autobiography of R.G. LeTourneau*, (1967: Chicago, Moody Publishers).

STILL SIGNING AUTOGRAPHS

"For someone who never played or coached a game, I think John Mark may have touched more Alabama fans than any other person ever did. Although he had limited abilities, Johnny made a difference with everyone he met. How much more of a difference can we make?"
Mal Moore – UA Athletic Director
(At John Mark Stallings funeral)

New Years Day, 1997 – Outback Bowl – Tampa, Florida: It had been a long, emotion-filled day for Alabama Head Football Coach Gene Stallings. His Crimson Tide team had earned a hard-fought 17-14 win over the University of Michigan and Stallings had just coached his final college football game.

It had been a difficult decision to leave the game after an almost forty-year coaching career. Still, Stallings was excited about returning to his ranch in Paris, Texas. After receiving hundreds of farewell handshakes and pats on the back from players, coaches, and fans, Stallings was anxious to leave the stadium. He boarded the team bus and took his customary seat on the front row.

After a several minute delay, Stallings turned to his administrative assistant, Gerald Jack, and asked what was causing the delay. "Coach, do you really want to know?" asked Jack. Stallings, irritated, snapped back, "Yes, of course, I want to know." Jack sheepishly whispered, "Coach, Johnny is still signing autographs." Coach Stallings chuckled, "I guess we can wait a little while longer."

John Mark "Johnny" Stallings was born at Tuscaloosa's Druid City Hospital on June 11, 1962. Stallings, a defensive assistant coach for Bear Bryant at the time, already had two lovely daughters. He was excited to have his little football player. "We've got the boy, Coach Bryant," Stallings proudly shouted into the hospital payphone.

The next day, the doctor informed Gene and his wife Ruth Ann that their baby had Down syndrome. When Stallings got the news, he fainted in the hospital hallway. He had imagined his son being a star football player like his daddy had been at Texas A&M. The news was shocking and devastating. Gene and Ruth Ann agonized about what they should do.

The doctors advised the Stallings to follow the accepted practice and institutionalize their son. Friends were concerned that keeping their son at home might adversely affect Stallings' coaching career. However, Gene and Ruth Ann decided to raise Johnny like any other little boy. And as Stallings' coaching career progressed, Johnny became his best friend and ever-present companion. He rarely missed a football practice or a game.

Stallings always made time for his special little buddy. Johnny was there by his side as Stallings' career took him from Alabama to Texas A&M, to the Dallas Cowboys, to the St. Louis Cardinals, and finally back to the University of Alabama. Johnny especially loved Alabama football. He stood proudly by his dad on the sidelines in New Orleans when Alabama beat the University of Miami 34-13 to win the National Championship in 1992.

Gene, Ruth Ann, and Johnny moved back to Paris, Texas, in 1997. Stallings worked long days on his ranch often with Johnny by his side. Johnny also worked at the local funeral home in town. Grieving families frequently requested that Johnny assist with their funerals because of his caring nature and concern. Johnny loved everybody and everybody loved Johnny.

Johnny suffered from congenital heart problems typically associated with Down syndrome. Coach Stallings always hoped that Johnny would outlive the old coach, but he didn't. John Mark Stallings died on August 2, 2008 at age forty-six.

Coach Stallings said of his beloved son:

I won a National Championship and coached in the Super Bowl, but Johnny was about as popular as I was. That's pretty good for a guy who couldn't count to ten, but who never forgot a name. When I coached, I had a whole lot less tolerance for the gifted and a whole lot more tolerance for the guy who wasn't quite as gifted. Johnny struggled to walk; he struggled to kick a ball and struggled with anything else he did. So I had a little more tolerance for those kinds of players.

The University of Alabama honored John Mark Stallings by naming the football complex equipment room in his honor. Johnny loved to spend time helping the training staff. There have been many great coaches, players, team physicians, and trainers who could have been honored in this way, but it is Johnny who will always be remembered for his love of the Alabama football program.

REFERENCES

Cecil Hurt, "John Mark Stallings dies," Tuscaloosa News, August 2, 2008, https://www.tuscaloosanews.com/article/DA/20080802/News/606115646/TL.

Gene Stallings and Sally Cook, *Another Season: A Coach's Story of Raising an Exceptional Son,* (1997: New York City, Little, Brown Publishing).

"John Mark Stallings, 1962-2008," RollTide.com, October 2, 2008, https://rolltide.com/news/2008/8/2/John_Mark_Stallings_1962_2008.

THE RELUCTANT
ARTIST

---

*"Many believe, and I believe, that I have
been designated for this work by God. In
spite of my old age, I do not want to give
it up. Lord, grant me that I may always
desire more that I can accomplish."*
Michelangelo

May 10, 1508 – Rome, Italy: When he had first been approached by Pope Julius II to tackle the project, he fled from his home in Caprese, Italy, to hide out in Rome rather than agree to the pope's request. He was overwhelmed by the magnitude of the task and he didn't think he was the right person for the job. After the second request from the pope, he reluctantly agreed to the contract.

He was a sculptor, not a painter, and this wasn't just any project. The pope wanted him to paint a series of murals in the Sistine Chapel—on the chapel ceiling, no less. The pope was adamant that Michelangelo di Lodovico Buonarroti Simoni—and no one else—was the right man for the job. Michelangelo felt he had no choice but to accept the assignment.

Michelangelo was born March 6, 1475 in Caprese, Italy. His mother died when he was six, and he went to live with the family of a stonecutter who worked in his father's marble quarry. The young lad was a natural with a chisel and hammer. Michelangelo was not a stonecutter; he was a sculptor, a prodigy with that rarest of abilities to see the angel within the marble. Among his early works was the *Pieta*, which was commissioned by the Vatican.

Michelangelo was thirty-three-years-old in July of 1508 when he began work on the Sistine Chapel ceiling. His only experience as a painter had occurred years before when he was a student. The pope wanted a depiction of biblical scenes from the New Testament but Michelangelo convinced him to use the book of Genesis as the subject matter.

The daunting mission was to paint more than 300 life-size figures on the curved ceiling, beginning with the creation of Adam and culminating with Noah and the flood. The ceiling spanned 130 feet long and 43 feet wide, a total of more than 5,600 square feet.

Because the pope was unwilling to suspend mass, Michelangelo's first challenge was to design a unique scaffold that could hinge off the walls beneath the 65-foot ceiling. Through trial and error, he learned the art of buon fresco painting, the technique of painting on a moist, plaster surface with colors ground up in limewater. In the early stages of the project, mold grew in the plaster and the painting had to be removed and redone.

The tedious painting required Michelangelo to stand on a scaffold, painting awkwardly above his head. His arms burned and ached from hours of holding the brush above his head. At other times, he painted with his back bent for long periods. His face and eyes provided a human canvas for the paint droppings. Michelangelo's initial fears became a reality. The task overwhelmed him. He dreaded the days when the impetuous pope climbed up on the scaffold to chastise him about his slow progress.

Michelangelo wondered why he'd agreed to this project. In his journal he wrote: "I am not in the right place—I am not a painter," but assisted by a team that mixed his paints and plaster and carried it up to the scaffold, Michelangelo painted on day after day. With his vision permanently affected by the strain and splatter, he made the final brush stroke in October 1512 more than four years after he had begun.

Five hundred years later, Michelangelo's magnificent painting of nine scenes from the Book of Genesis is the crowning masterpiece of the European Renaissance. His fresco of the creation of Adam is second in popularity only to Leonardo da Vinci's *Mona Lisa*. Five million visitors tour the Sistine Chapel each year and stand in awe at Michelangelo's brilliant creation. Pope Julius II was right—Michelangelo was the right man for the mission.

REFERENCES

"How Michelangelo Painted the Sistine Chapel," Great Names in History, Published July 25, 2010, https://100falcons.wordpress.com/2010/07/25/how-michelangelo-painted-the-sistine-chapel.

"Michelangelo Paints the Sistine Chapel," EyeWitness to History, 2005, http://www.eyewitnesstohistory.com/michelangelo.

"Michelangelo's Painting of the Sistine Chapel Ceiling," ItalianRenaissance.org, Published May 9, 2013, http://www.italianrenaissance.org/a-closer-look-michelangelos-painting-of-the-sistine-chapel-ceiling.

Wikipedia, "Michelangelo," Last updated October 13, 2020, https://en.wikipedia.org/wiki/Michelangelo.

NO GOING BACK

"A single feat of daring can alter the whole conception of what is possible."
Graham Greene

May 21, 1927 – Paris, France: Forty miles from Le Bourget Airfield, he began to see the flares. Less than thirty-three hours earlier, 500 people had watched the twetny-five-year-old pilot take off from a muddy Roosevelt Field runway in New York. He hoped to become the first pilot to make a solo non-stop flight to Paris.

As the airplane dropped toward the runway, he saw the throngs of people—a scene that would remain with him for a lifetime. One hundred thousand cheering people had surrounded the airport awaiting his arrival. Charles Lindberg had become a world hero.

Lindberg, born one year before the Wright Brothers' historic first flight in 1903, fell in love with the idea of flying. While studying engineering at the University of Wisconsin, he dropped out of school to chase his dream.

After two years of Army pilot training, he got a job flying mail from Chicago to St. Louis.

In 1919, Raymond Ortieg, a New York hotel owner, offered $25,000 to the first pilot to fly solo non-stop between New York and Paris. By 1925, several pilots had died trying, but no one had claimed Ortieg's prize. Lindberg pledged his life savings of $2,000 and was able to convince several St. Louis businessmen to donate $15,000 for his attempt.

The four biggest airplane builders in the United States turned Lindberg down. He found a small company in San Diego, California, to specially design an airplane for his trip. To reduce the weight of the plane and accommodate more gasoline, Lindberg choose to forego the heavy pilot seat, the radio, and a parachute.

Lindberg's chief concerns included engine reliability, running out of fuel, and navigational error, but his biggest worry was pilot fatigue. Thirteen days before his flight, two World War I French aviators took off from Paris en route for New York and were never heard from again.

Undeterred, on May 20, 1927, after two days of weather delays, Lindberg took off at 7:52 a.m. from the 5,000-foot runway at Roosevelt field. With 2,700 pounds of fuel in a 2,500-pound plane, he needed every foot of the runway to clear the telephone lines which were his first hurdle.

Lindberg used a simple altimeter to determine altitude, a compass and a stopwatch to navigate his course, and he made pencil marks on the gas tanks to track fuel levels. Benefitting from good weather, he maintained a speed of 100 miles per hour and an altitude less than 500 feet and reached Newfoundland at 6 p.m.

At 9 p.m., a thunderstorm forced him to climb to 10,000 feet to fly above the storm. With ice forming on the wings, he feared the plane would become too heavy to fly. "The ice forming worried me a great deal," recalled Lindberg. "And I debated whether I should keep going or go back. I decided I must not think any more about going back."

At 2 a.m. with daylight dawning, Lindberg calculated that he was halfway to Paris. He had another eighteen hours to go. Rather than excitement, he felt only dread. At 5 a.m., dense fog forced him to fly ten feet above the ocean to maintain visual contact. He repeatedly nodded off waking seconds, sometimes minutes later. Finally, after flying for hours, the fog cleared, and he spotted several small fishing boats. At twenty-seven hours into the mission, Lindberg had made it to the coast of Ireland. He was now wide-awake.

At 10:22 p.m. Paris time, thirty-three and a half hours and 3,597 miles after leaving New York, Lindberg's plane *The Spirit of St. Louis* touched down at Le Bourget Airfield. He had not slept in fifty-five hours.

The huge crowd stormed the barricades and pulled the weary pilot from his plane. They paraded him around the field on their shoulders before taking him to the awaiting press corp. Twenty-four years after the Wright brothers' fifty-nine-second flight, Charles Lindberg daringly secured his place in aviation history, and it opened the door to transcontinental flights between America and Europe.

REFERENCES

"Charles Lindberg Biography; Flight Log, and Timeline" pages, Charles Lindberg, Accessed November 23, 2020, www.charleslindberg.com.

George Petras, "Charles Lindberg and the epic flight of the Spirit of St. Louis," USA Today, May 20, 2017, https://www.usatoday.com/pages/interactives/spirit-of-st-louis-anniversary.

THE KANSAS FLYER

"When the race seems lost, when the odds appear unbeatable, when the pain is too much...never quit."
Glenn Cunningham

February 9, 1917 – Sunflower School – Elkhart, Kansas: Glenn Cunningham, age seven, and his thirteen-year-old brother, Floyd, walked two miles to the one-room school. Floyd prepared to light a fire in the large pot-bellied stove as he did most winter mornings to warm the building. He loaded the wood into the stove and doused the logs with what he thought was kerosene, but the fuel container had been mistakenly filled with gasoline.

When he lit the match, the stove exploded engulfing both boys in flames. Glenn survived, but was burned on more than fifty percent of his body, mostly below the waist. Floyd died several days later. The fire burned the flesh off his knees and shins, and the toes on his left foot were completely burned off. "Glenn might live, if he doesn't get an infection," the doctor advised, "But he'll never walk again, he is too badly burned."

When the doctor left, Glenn cried, "I will walk. I will walk." His mother kissed his forehead and whispered, "I know you will. He is wrong." Glenn got an infection a week later and the doctor recommended both his legs be amputated. His mother refused. She had lost one son and would not allow her other son to lose his legs.

Glenn survived the infection, but his recovery was long and painful. Unable to straighten his legs due to the scar tissue, Glenn learned to stand by pulling up on the back of a chair. Each day his mother would push his wheelchair outside where he would practice pulling up on a fence and walking along the posts for hours. Ten months after the tragedy, on Christmas Eve 1917, he took his first unassisted steps. In time, Glenn discovered it was less painful to run than to walk.

At age twelve, Glenn won his first racing medal at school. During his senior year of high school, he set the Kansas state record for the mile at the state championship meet with a time of 4:28. A few months later in Chicago, Glenn broke the national high school record with a 4:24 mile, earning him the distinction of the greatest high school miler in history.

A decade after the doctor wanted to amputate his legs, Glenn signed a track scholarship with the University of Kansas. Dubbed the "Kansas Flyer," he set numerous records during his college track days including a world record mile of 4:06 minutes. In the 1936 Berlin Olympics, he broke the world record for the 1500-meter run, missing the gold by a fraction of a second, but winning the Silver Medal for the USA.

Later in 1938, Glenn broke the world record for the indoor mile with a time of 4:04 and set his sights on winning the gold medal in the mile in the 1940 Olympics. When World War II caused the cancelation of the 1940 Olympics, he retired from track.

After earning a bachelors and master's degree from the University of Kansas, Glenn Cunningham received his PhD in physical education from New York University in 1938. He was Director of Physical Education at Cornell College in Iowa for several years before he resigned and with the help of his wife started the Glenn Cunningham Youth Ranch in Kansas. The 900-acre ranch provided a home for orphans and children from troubled backgrounds. Through this program, the Cunningham's helped raise more than 9,000 children during a 30-year period.

The seven-year-old boy who was told he would never walk again broke the world record for the mile and the 1500-meter run on seven different occasions. In 1974, the United States Track and Field Federation inducted Glenn Cunningham into its inaugural Hall of Fame class. In 1978, a decade after his death, Madison Square Garden in New York City recognized him as the most outstanding track athlete to perform in the building over the course of its first one hundred years.

REFERENCES

Darryl Hicks, "Glenn Cunningham (1908-1988)...Never Quit," My Best Years, Accessed November 22, 2020, http://www.mybestyears.com/InterviewSpotlights/CUNNINGHAMGlenn080409.

Encyclopedia Britannica Editors, "Glenn Cunningham," Britannica, Last updated July 31, 2020, https://www.britannica.com/biography/Glenn-Cunningham.

Mark D. Hersey, "Cunningham Calls It A Career," KU History, April 20, 1940, https://kuhistory.ku.edu/articles/cunningham-calls-it-career.

WILLIAM AND THE WINDMILL

"In this life you can go through many difficulties, but if you know what you want to do, and if you focus and work, then in the end you will end up doing it. No matter what happens, if you don't give up, you will still succeed."
William Kamkwamba

2002 – Mastala Village, Milawi, Africa: The people in his African village called him "Misala," the crazy one. The first time William Kamkwamba saw a picture of a windmill, he was in a small library in the neighboring village of Wimbe. The fifteen-year-old wasn't entirely sure what it was, or how it worked, but a dream was born that day to build a wind machine for his village.

William was born in Malawi in southeast Africa. With an annual average income of $160, it is one of the ten poorest and least-developed countries in the world. His father, like most men in the village, made his living farming a small plot of corn and tobacco with a hoe. There was no electricity or running water in their small thatched-roof, dirt-floor hut. The family diet consisted of a porridge made from corn and an occasional chicken at Christmas.

William dropped out of school in the ninth grade because his family could not pay the tuition. Later that year, after neighbors died from starvation in yet another severe drought, he decided to try to make his wind machine dream into a reality. Inspired by both hunger and poor lighting from the kerosene lamps in his hut, William regularly walked the three miles to the Wimbe library to learn more about the wind machine featured in the eighth grade textbook *Using Energy*.

He scavenged around his village for building materials and found a broken bicycle, a tractor fan blade, and an old shock absorber. In a neighboring village, he unearthed an old car battery that he would use to store the electricity. He cut down blue gum trees to fashion as the legs for his wind machine.

Using a flathead screwdriver, the only tool that he owned, William began to assemble his invention as the neighbors watched and worried about his machine. They feared his strange electric wind invention would cause bad magic, resulting in more drought and famine in their land. William's father and mother shared these concerns. "Why didn't William act like the other boys his age and help his father with the farming?" they wondered.

After many failed attempts, William's fifteen-foot tall windmill finally worked. It generated enough electricity to operate two light bulbs and two small transistor radios. Encouraged by his success, William built a solar-powered water pump to supply the first drinking water to the village and he made two other windmills, the tallest thirty-nine feet, to supply power for the small village.

The windmills drew visitors from miles around the village. Malawi government officials came to see William's strange wind machine. The story quickly spread around the world. In December 2007, *The Wall Street Journal* featured William Kamkwamba and his inventions. That same year, several wealthy businessmen agreed to pay for William's education. He enrolled in an intensive two-year academic program combining Cambridge University's curriculum with leadership, entrepreneurship, and African studies at the African Leadership Academy in Johannesburg, South Africa.

In 2010, William was one of four recipients of the prestigious GO Ingenuity Award, a prize awarded to inventors to promote the sharing of their innovations and skills with youth in developing nations. In 2014, William graduated from Dartmouth College, one of America's top universities. He has returned to Malawi and is working on other inventions to help his country. Those in Mastala no longer consider William Kamkwamba the crazy man—he is a national hero.

REFERENCES

Christy O'Keefe, "'Boy who harnessed the wind' comes to College," The Dartmouth, Thayer School of Engineering at Dartmouth, October 19, 2009, https://engineering.dartmouth.edu/news/boy-who-harnessed-the-wind-comes-to-college.

"Malawian innovator and author William Kamkwamba working with WiderNet to bridge the know-do gap," UNC School of Information and Library Science, May 4, 2016, https://sils.unc.edu/news/2016/Kamkwamba.

Sangwani Mwafulirwa, "School dropout with a streak genius," *Malawi Premier Daily,* November 20, 2006.

Wikipedia, "William Kamkwamba," Last updated October 28, 2020, https://en.wikipedia.org/wiki/William_Kamkwamba.

Pete Black, a retired civil engineer turned writer, hails from Monroeville, Alabama, home of literary icons Harper Lee, Truman Capote, and Pulitzer-Prize-winning journalist Cynthia Tucker. He has written a weekly column, Heart Matters, in the Monroe Journal since 2012 and his short stories have been published in the GreyThoughts Writer's Club as well as in Spillwords Publishing.